LEADERS OF THE SCIENTIFIC REVOLUTION™

GALILEO GALILEI

Corona Brezina

Rosen YA

New York

Published in 2018 by The Rosen Publishing Group, Inc.
29 East 21st Street, New York, NY 10010

Copyright © 2018 by The Rosen Publishing Group, Inc.

First Edition

All rights reserved. No part of this book may be reproduced in any form without permission in writing from the publisher, except by a reviewer.

Library of Congress Cataloging-in-Publication Data

Names: Brezina, Corona, author.
Title: Galileo Galilei / Corona Brezina.
Description: First edition. | New York: Rosen Publishing, 2018. | Series: Leaders of the scientific revolution | Audience: Grades 7 to 12. | Includes bibliographical references and index.
Identifiers: LCCN 2016053794 | ISBN 9781508174684 (library bound)
Subjects: LCSH: Galilei, Galileo, 1564–1642—Juvenile literature. | Astronomers—Italy—Biography—Juvenile literature. | Physicists—Italy—Biography—Juvenile literature.
Classification: LCC QB36.G2 B638 2018 | DDC 520.92 [B] —dc23
LC record available at https://lccn.loc.gov/2016053794

Manufactured in China

On the cover: This portrait of Italian mathematician, scientist, and astronomer Galileo Galilei (1564–1642) was painted in the seventeenth century. *Background*: This page from Galileo's 1613 book *Istoria e dimostrazioni intorno alle macchie solari e loro accidenti (History and demonstrations concerning sunspots and their properties)* shows the changes in sunspots that he observed.

CONTENTS

INTRODUCTION 4

CHAPTER ONE
GALILEO'S EARLY LIFE 8

CHAPTER TWO
MATHEMATICS, MECHANICS, AND MOTION 23

CHAPTER THREE
PEERING THROUGH THE TELESCOPE 39

CHAPTER FOUR
COPERNICANISM AND CONTROVERSY 54

CHAPTER FIVE
THE *DIALOGUE* AND CONDEMNATION 69

CHAPTER SIX
***TWO NEW SCIENCES* AND GALILEO'S LEGACY** ... 84

TIMELINE 95
GLOSSARY 97
FOR MORE INFORMATION 100
FOR FURTHER READING 104
BIBLIOGRAPHY 106
INDEX 108

INTRODUCTION

On June 22, 1633, a frail sixty-nine-year-old man was led to the great hall at the church of Santa Maria Sopra Minerva in Rome, Italy. Dressed in penitential white clothing, he had been released from confinement earlier in the morning. A crowd of Catholic clergy was assembled to watch the proceedings. The accused knelt before his judges to hear their findings on the charge of heresy—doctrines contradicting church teachings.

The old man was the acclaimed astronomer Galileo Galilei. He was awaiting the ruling on his trial for the crime of teaching Copernicanism, the

Introduction

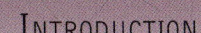

An 1847 painting depicts the condemnation of Galileo Galilei in 1632 by the Catholic Church. The trial and sentencing served to silence Galileo's defense of the theories of Copernicus.

theory that the earth revolves around the sun. According to the contemporary Catholic Church, the earth was the stationary center of the universe around which all heavenly bodies orbited. Official condemnation was about to silence Galileo on the troublesome topic forever.

At last, the judgment and sentence were announced. Galileo was found vehemently suspected of heresy—a clear verdict of guilty. He was sentenced to indefinite imprisonment, and his book advocating Copernicanism was banned. But the humiliation was not complete. He was required to abjure, or publicly renounce, his controversial views. He read out a statement acknowledging that he had erred, and swore on the Bible that he would never again repeat his heresy.

A story exists claiming that after finishing the statement, he muttered as an aside, "And yet, it moves." Historians agree that this incident is a myth. Even so, some of Galileo's most important scientific work served to prove that the earth does indeed move.

Galileo had stunned the world with the astronomical discoveries he made using his new instrument, the telescope. He showed that moons orbited Jupiter. The moon had mountains and valleys. Sunspots periodically flared on the surface of the sun.

Galileo's astronomical achievements brought him fame, and few people gazing through the telescope could deny the evidence before their own eyes. Nevertheless, his observations led him to conclusions that conflicted with the conventionally accepted model of the universe. When he persisted in publicizing his theories about the earth orbiting the sun, the Catholic Church moved to condemn him.

Today, Galileo is considered one of the key figures of the Scientific Revolution. In addition to his astronomical breakthroughs, Galileo improved the design of the telescope, invented many other mechanical devices and instruments, and made new discoveries in physics. His work helped science make the transition from the medieval age to the modern.

CHAPTER ONE

Galileo's Early Life

Galileo Galilei was born in Pisa, Italy, on February 15, 1564. His father, Vincenzo Galilei, was a highly regarded musician from Florence, the capital of the Grand Duchy of Tuscany, who played the lute. His mother, Giulia Ammananti, came from a respectable family of cloth merchants. After their marriage in 1562, they settled down in her hometown of Pisa. In accordance with a Tuscan custom, their eldest son was given the first name "Galileo" that was a variant form of the family name, "Galilei." Later in life, after he became famous, Galileo would refer to himself by his first name only, as is the common practice today.

Vincenzo Galilei was a performer and teacher, but today, he is best remembered for his study of music theory. He advocated revolutionary ideas about harmony

Pisa, seen here in a sixteenth-century print, was ruled from afar by Cosimo de' Medici, grand duke of Florence. Cosimo rejuvenated the town through public works projects and support of learning and the arts.

and tuning that challenged musical conventions of the day. Vincenzo even conducted experiments that tested the properties of lute strings, such as how the tension of different materials affected musical pitch. Galileo probably helped his father in this experimentation.

THE MEDICIS OF FLORENCE

Florence in Galileo's time was the capital of the Grand Duchy of Tuscany, an independent state located in west-central Italy and ruled by a branch of the powerful Medici family. The Medicis attained their vast wealth through banking and trade. The first grand duke was Cosimo I de' Medici, who took the title in 1569. The Medicis were renowned supporters of the arts—Vincenzo Galilei largely made his living at the grand duke's court. Galileo himself would be supported by Cosimo's eventual successors, Cosimo II and Ferdinando II. But Ferdinando ruled during a period of economic decline, and Medici control of Florence ended in 1737. One of the final acts of the last grand duke, Gian Gastone, was to memorialize Galileo in Florence's Basilica di Santa Croce, sometimes called the "Temple of the Italian Glories" for the notable figures buried there.

Vincenzo taught his son to play the lute, and Galileo acquired a lifelong love of music. Significantly, Galileo also followed the example set by his father, who had a tendency to question authority.

In 1572, Vincenzo returned to Florence to work under the patronage of a Florentine count. His family joined him two years later. Galileo had six younger siblings, although only two sisters and a brother reached adulthood.

The next year, his father sent the eleven-year-old Galileo to be educated at a Benedictine monastery, Santa Maria di Vallombrosa, in an isolated valley southeast of Florence. At Vallombrosa, which was a renowned institution of learning, he studied subjects such as Greek, Latin, logic, philosophy, literature, religion, mathematics, and science. The monks recognized that the boy was exceptionally gifted intellectually, and Galileo thrived in the austere and scholarly atmosphere of the monastery. After a couple of years, he announced that he wished to join the order. Vincenzo was horrified. He did not want his son to become a monk. In 1579, he made the journey to Vallombrosa and brought Galileo home to Florence.

The Galileis lived in a small house, and having another person to feed and maintain was a financial burden for the impoverished family. Galileo was sent away to learn the wool trade from a cousin, a merchant in Pisa. When he was old enough, he enrolled in the University of Pisa.

GALILEO'S INTELLECTUAL ORIGINS

Throughout his life, Galileo proudly considered himself a Florentine—a citizen of the city of Florence—despite

Galileo Galilei

Galileo received his earliest formal education at the ancient abbey at Vallombrosa, where monks taught students and followed their own scholarly pursuits.

his Pisan childhood and many years spent living elsewhere. Galileo's father was descended from Florentine nobility, and both Vincenzo and Galileo described themselves as Florentine gentlemen.

Galileo's Early Life

Florence had been a significant center of the Italian Renaissance, the flowering of arts, culture, and learning that began in the 1300s. The Renaissance, which means "rebirth" or "reawakening," followed the Middle Ages and inspired many innovations and achievements in scholarship and art. The invention of the printing press made written works more widely available than ever before, and demand for books increased. By the time of Galileo's birth, however, the spirit of the Renaissance was in decline in Florence. The authorities began to ban some literary works and curtail the free exchange of ideas. Still, Galileo possessed a range of knowledge and interests that embodied the legacy of the Renaissance—in addition to science and mathematics, Galileo was accomplished in the fields of music, poetry, art, philosophy, and writing.

Greek and Latin texts were still at the core of the intellectual worldview of Galileo's time. Professors delivered lectures in Latin, which was the language used by scholars across Europe. Students learned from works written more than a thousand years earlier. The writings of the ancient Greek mathematician Euclid (born circa 300 BCE), for example, were central to the study of mathematics.

The ideas of Archimedes (circa 287–212 BCE) were highly influential in mathematics, physics, and engineering. But the undisputed ultimate authority on knowledge of all types, including physical science, was the ancient Greek philosopher and scientist Aristotle (384–322 BCE).

Today, the term "Aristotelianism" refers primarily to Aristotle's philosophical movement. During Galileo's lifetime, however, Aristotelianism described the systems of the natural world as well as abstract concepts. His "natural philosophy," as the physical sciences were

Galileo's Early Life

This panoramic view of Florence was made in 1490. Galileo always felt that his real home was Tuscany's capital of Florence, the seat of the Italian Renaissance and a prosperous port city.

called, included topics such as physics, biology, chemistry, zoology, and meteorology. Aristotle established the rules governing his natural systems using observations and logic. In some areas, such as biology, Aristotle's work laid a solid foundation for studying the field. In others, such as physics, later experiments and observations would largely disprove Aristotle's ideas. Medieval and Renaissance scholars recognized that Aristotle was not correct in every detail, but most accepted the basic framework put forth in his writings. Instead of challenging the principles, they wrote extensive commentary and interpretation of Aristotelianism.

Aristotle's physics dealt with phenomena such as motion, time, and the nature of matter. These laws of physics governed his model of the natural order of the universe, or cosmology. Aristotle placed the stationary earth at the center of the cosmos. The earth, or terrestrial zone, was separated from the celestial heavens above. In the earthly realm, all bodies were made up of four basic elements: earth, fire, water, and air. These four elements tended to move to their natural place assigned to them in the cosmos. For example, bodies made of earth would sink toward the center of the earth, which was the center of the Aristotle's universe. Fire, by contrast, would rise.

Heavenly bodies in Aristotle's cosmology were composed of a substance called quintessence that was not found on the earth. Each body moved in circular orbits around the earth in separate crystalline spheres nested within each other. The moon occupied the nearest sphere, then the sun, other planets, and stars. The motions of the heavens were governed by a separate set of laws.

Subsequent advances in astronomy did not ques-

NICOLAUS COPERNICUS

Nicolaus Copernicus (1473–1543) was an astronomer who lived and worked in present-day Poland, although he studied in Italy during his youth. His life's work was the book *De Revolutionibus Orbium Coelestium* (*On the Revolutions of the Heavenly Spheres*), which was published in 1543 as Copernicus lay on his deathbed. Unlike previous approaches, Copernicus's model represented a coherent system that explained the observed motion of the planets.

Copernicus had presented his theory as a true explanation of how the universe works. However, without Copernicus's knowledge, the printer added a preface stating that the Copernican system was merely a theoretical model intended to make astronomical calculations easier. For this reason, the work created little controversy upon release. The heliocentric model did not become widely debated until it gained the support of astronomers such as Galileo and Johannes Kepler (1571–1630) many decades later.

tion the geocentric, or earth-centered, model of the universe. The astronomer Ptolemy, who lived during the second century CE, created a catalog of stars and developed mathematical means of calculating the positions of heavenly bodies. But his findings fit within the framework of Aristotle's cosmology.

Finally, in the sixteenth century, the astronomer Nicolaus Copernicus developed a cosmological model that rejected the Aristotelian system. He used mathematical calculations to support the theory that the sun was at the center of the universe, called the heliocentric

Copernicus's heliocentric model of the universe, represented here, accounted for the irregular observed motion of the planets and their variations in brightness, which could not be explained in Aristotle's model.

model. The earth is a planet that revolves around the sun along with the other planets.

Copernicus's contemporaries were reluctant to adopt the new model. It required that they reject Aristotelian physics outright—a daunting prospect. Intuitively, Copernicus's theory was hard to accept, because he was asking them to believe that the ground under their feet was in constant motion. For decades after Copernicus's death, his theories failed to attract serious attention from scholars.

Today, Copernicus is recognized as one of the first major figures of what is now called the Scientific Revolution. This era, which generally encompassed the sixteenth, seventeenth, and part of the eighteenth centuries, ushered in new scientific discoveries as well as new means of approaching science. Experiments would use the scientific method and seek out practical applications of science. Galileo, along with other scientists and philosophers such as Francis Bacon (1561–1626) and René Descartes (1596–1650), helped introduce these new ways of thinking that would supplant Aristotle's worldview.

AN INTERRUPTED EDUCATION

In the summer of 1581, the seventeen-year-old Galileo enrolled in the University of Pisa. In accordance with his father's wishes, he began studying medicine. One of his ancestors, the Galileo Galilei who was the founder of his family, had been a renowned doctor. In addition, Vincenzo appreciated that medicine was a secure and lucrative career.

The University of Pisa was a highly regarded institution with more than six hundred students. It offered courses in theology, law, and the arts. Most of the subjects taught by the "arts" faculty were related to the study of medicine. Beginning medical students studied natural philosophy and medical topics such as the physiology of Galen, the great Greek physician and philosopher of the second century CE. Mathematics was considered a minor subject of interest. The mathematics lecturer at the university focused on astrology, because doctors routinely cast horoscopes to determine medical outcomes and discover the appropriate treatment.

Galileo first began to question the Aristotelian system during his time at Pisa. He gained a reputation for challenging his professors. Once, he used the example of hail to cast doubt on Aristotle's physics. According to Aristotle, larger, heavier bodies fell more quickly than smaller, lighter ones. Why then, Galileo asked, did hailstones of different sizes fall at the same time? His teachers were unable to provide a satisfactory explanation.

Galileo's Early Life

Galileo may have been inspired to investigate the motion of pendulums after observing a flickering oil lamp swinging during Mass in the drafty cathedral of Pisa, which is seen here.

Galileo found himself more drawn to mathematics than medicine. In 1583, he sneaked into lectures given at the Medici Court by Ostilio Ricci, the official court mathematician. Galileo immersed himself in mathematics, mastering Euclid's work on geometry, the *Elements,* largely on his own. Galileo began skipping lectures and neglecting his medical studies as he concentrated on mathematics, hiding his interest in the subject from his father.

Disturbed, Vincenzo traveled to Pisa to check on Galileo. Ricci recognized Galileo's talent and urged Vincenzo to allow him to study mathematics rather than medicine. Vincenzo was torn. He held mathematics in respect, but the field of medicine offered financial security. He remained undecided for a year, and meanwhile, Ricci tutored Galileo in secret. He introduced Galileo to the works of Archimedes, which came as a revelation. Finally, Vincenzo consented to Galileo studying mathematics.

According to one story, Galileo's first major scientific achievement occurred in 1583 when he was attending church in the Pisa Cathedral and observed the swinging motion of a chandelier. He recognized that the oscillation could be used to measure time. At this point, the pendulum had not yet been invented. Galileo experimented with weights attached to different lengths of string. He also showed his pendulum to his professors at the university, demonstrating that it could be used to measure a patient's pulse rate. However, some historians consider this incident a myth.

In 1585, Vincenzo informed Galileo that he could no longer afford to pay for his schooling. Galileo left the University of Pisa without completing his degree.

CHAPTER TWO

MATHEMATICS, MECHANICS, AND MOTION

Galileo spent the first half of his career—from 1589 to 1610—as a mathematics professor. During this time, he also tackled what would today be considered physics and engineering problems, such as studying the nature of motion and inventing mechanical devices. Although he sometimes felt discouraged as he endeavored to establish himself in the field of mathematics, he achieved professional success and prosperity by the turn of the century. He spent most of his teaching career at the University of Padua, and he would later recall those years as the happiest of his life.

He made some of his most important scientific discoveries during these years, which were also crucial to the development of his intellectual convictions, especially on the topic of Copernicanism. Yet, only a sparse historical record exists of these years before Galileo became prominent. The outline of his life is well known, but historians are mostly left guessing about the insights that led to the evolution of his scientific views.

ESTABLISHING A REPUTATION

After returning to Florence in 1585, Galileo devoted himself to the study of mathematics. He earned a meager living by lecturing on mathematics and tutoring private students, occasionally traveling for teaching jobs in the Tuscan town of Siena and at his former school at Vallambrosa. He also helped his father with experiments in music. But there was not much demand for his expertise.

Galileo considered Archimedes a genius, and during this period, he explored the implications of one of Archimedes's most famous discoveries. Archimedes was given the challenge of determining whether a crown was made of solid gold without melting it down. Supposedly, the great mathematician once jumped out of the bathtub shouting "Eureka!" when he observed the changing water level. He had realized that by placing the crown in water and measuring the displacement of water, he could determine whether it was pure gold or diluted with a metal such as silver. Galileo devised a new method of determining weight based on Archimedes's principles. He conceived of a highly precise scale, or balance, which determined weight by balancing the object

Mathematics, Mechanics, and Motion

Galileo was an ardent follower of Archimedes, the greatest mathematician and inventor of ancient Greece. His works greatly influenced many scientists of the Renaissance.

against a counterweight first in air, then in water, and then comparing the difference. He described his instrument in his first notable work, *La Bilancetta* (*The Little Balance*), published in 1586.

Galileo's goal was to obtain a university position. He recognized that he'd need influential supporters to promote his case. He sent examples of his examination of Archimedes's work to the renowned mathematician Christopher Clavius, hoping for a recommendation for an open post at the University of Bologna. Clavius had written works on mathematics and astronomy that were highly regarded, and he had contributed to reforms that created the Gregorian calendar, which is still used today. In 1587, Galileo traveled to Rome to visit the eminent mathematician, and they remained regular correspondents for years afterward. Nevertheless, Galileo did not win the Bologna post.

His next hope was that Francesco de' Medici, the grand duke of the Tuscan court, might assist him. But Francesco died suddenly in 1587, and his successor, Ferdinando (also known as Ferdinand I), did not share his brother's interest in natural science. However, Galileo succeeded in attracting the attention of the mathematician Marquis Guidobaldo del Monte, a nobleman who would become Galileo's longtime friend and supporter. Guidobaldo could provide a connection to the grand duke of Tuscany.

In 1588 or 1589, Galileo was invited to lecture at Florence's prestigious Academy. The topic was both

Mathematics, Mechanics, and Motion

In addition to being Galileo's patron and friend, the Marquis Guidobaldo del Monte was a notable mathematician, engineer, and astronomer who wrote an influential book on mechanics.

GALILEO GALILEI

A painting by Sandro Botticelli depicts the circles of hell as described in Dante's *Inferno*. Galileo approached the topic as a mathematician and scientist while lecturing before the Academy.

literary and mathematic—he was to describe the location, size, and shape of hell as depicted in the *Inferno*, the first part of the long narrative poem *The Divine Comedy*, by the Italian poet Dante (1265–1321). Galileo described the Inferno as funnel-shaped, and he used mathematical clues in the text to determine dimen-

Mathematics, Mechanics, and Motion

sions. The lectures were well received, bringing public recognition to the little-known young mathematician.

RETURN TO PISA

In 1589, Galileo won an appointment to the chair of mathematics at the University of Pisa. He achieved the position with the support of the Marquis del Monte as well as recognition of his own abilities. Galileo's duties included teaching Euclid's *Elements*, astronomy, and astrology. Still, the Pisa professorship was not Galileo's dream job. The post was only for three years and it paid poorly—the annual salary of sixty florins a month was paltry. By contrast, the philosophy professor Jacopo Mazzoni, who became Galileo's friend, was paid 700 florins.

When Galileo arrived at Pisa, he discovered that Mazzoni and some other professors were vigorously debating the nature of motion. The philosophy professor Girolamo Borro, a staunch Aristotelian, had written a work on the motion of heavy and light bodies. According to one story, Galileo joined the dispute by dropping objects off the top of the Leaning Tower of Pisa. His objective was to test Aristotle's notion that heavier bodies fell faster than lighter ones. A large crowd assembled to watch Galileo toss out various spheres made of different sizes and materials. The demonstration disproved Aristotle's prediction that the heavier object would fall significantly faster, but Galileo did not have the means to make precise measurements of the disparity.

Galileo began writing his own work on motion shortly after arriving in Pisa. It examined bodies in free fall as well as the paths of projectiles and the speed of balls rolling down an incline. *De Motu* (*On Motion*) did not bring any significant new insights to the debate, although it did introduce key concepts that Galileo would address in later works. Galileo never published it.

Galileo antagonized many of the professors and administrators at the university during his time at Pisa. He was argumentative and made no effort to hide his contempt for his traditionalist colleagues. Notoriously, he mocked the academic clothing worn by professors, flowing robes that resembled a toga. He was even fined for failing to wear it. Galileo solidified his unpopularity by writing a witty three-hundred-line poem lampooning the garment and its social significance. His contract was not renewed when it ran out in 1592.

Vincenzo Galilei died in 1591, and Galileo now had to support his family financially. His sister Virginia had recently married, but their father had not been able to provide the full amount of her dowry. Therefore, Galileo would have to pay the rest of the money in installments. He was also responsible for the living expenses of his mother and young sister, Livia, as well as for music lessons for his brother, Michelangelo.

In 1592, Galileo applied for a position as professor of mathematics at the prestigious University of Padua. He enlisted the support of the del Monte family, who put him in touch with contacts in Padua. He traveled to Venice and befriended Giovanni Pinelli, an influential nobleman and intellectual at the heart of the Paduan cultural scene. Pinelli coached Galileo on his meeting with the three examiners, who subsequently recommended him for the job. Finally, as a Florentine subject, he needed Grand Duke Ferdinando's permission to leave Tuscany. It was granted without objection. Galileo was appointed to the post. He even beat out fellow mathematician Antonio Magini, who had been chosen over Galileo years earlier for a position at the University of Bologna.

PROFESSORSHIP AT PADUA

The University of Padua was the second oldest university in Italy, after the University of Bologna. Its mathematics department, as well, was second only to that of Bologna. Students came from across Italy and abroad to study at the institution. For a time, an exiled prince of

Sweden stayed with Galileo, who tutored the prince in the Italian language.

Galileo gave his inaugural lecture on December 7, 1592. By tradition, new professors presented a formal lecture on their subject in Latin to the university community. Because Galileo spoke from memory, there is no record of his specific topic. But his fiery presentation drew widespread praise, and the leading scientists of the time took note. Tycho Brahe of Denmark, the most famous living astronomer, praised Galileo.

Galileo lived with Pinelli for a time before he found his own lodgings. Here, he met some of the leading intellectuals of the city, who gathered at Pinelli's house for wide-ranging debates and discussions on culture, learning, and politics. Galileo's Paduan circle included scholars who challenged established doctrines. The friar Paolo Sarpi was a philosopher with a deep knowledge of natural science and mathematics. In 1606, he would become known across Europe for supporting Venice in a dispute with Pope Paul V. Tommaso Campanella was a philosopher and astrologer who wrote the controversial work *Philosophia Sensibus Demonstrata* (Philosophy Demonstrated by the Senses) and eventually spent twenty-seven years imprisoned for his unorthodox views. Galileo may have met philosopher and mathematician Giordano Bruno (1548–1600) at this time, as Bruno held a position at Padua for a few months during Galileo's early tenure.

GIORDANO BRUNO

The trial and execution of Giordano Bruno stood as a cautionary example for any of the scholars in Galileo's circle who were tempted by new ideas and innovations. A philosopher, mathematician, astronomer, and a Dominican priest until 1576, Bruno held radical views that went beyond Copernicanism. He believed in an infinite universe with an infinite number of worlds supporting intelligent life. Bruno also wrote about magic and the occult. In Venice in 1592, he was denounced to the Inquisition—the arm of the Catholic Church charged with investigating and punishing heresy. He was thrown into jail and held for eight years as the trial dragged on. Eventually, Cardinal Robert Bellarmine, a leading authority on theological controversies, accused Bruno of a list of eight heresies. He was judged a heretic in 1600, and Bellarmine signed his death warrant. Bruno was burned at the stake in the heart of Rome.

Galileo's academic responsibilities included instructing students on topics such as geometry and astronomy. He became known as a brilliant lecturer. He also was constantly in need of money, as his income of 180 florins a year was still too small to cover his responsibilities to his family. He tutored students and gave lectures on a wide range of subjects to earn extra money. He sometimes took students into his house as boarders. Nonetheless, his financial troubles persisted. In 1593, he was nearly arrested for missing payments on his sister's dowry.

Galileo put his mathematical and mechanical abilities to good practical use, inventing mechanical devices and consulting on engineering problems. He wrote a treatise on mechanical devices and another on military fortifications, probably at the request of Francesco del Monte, who was a general of the Venetian infantry. He also privately taught students on military fortifications and other topics.

Shortly after Galileo arrived in Padua, Giacomo Contarini, the superintendent of the Arsenal of Venice, approached him with a different problem related to military defense. The Arsenal was the complex of shipyards at the heart of the city's shipbuilding industry. Contarini asked Galileo for suggestions to improve the design of the ships that defended Venice. Galileo gave advice on the placement of the oars, producing a design that treated them as levers.

His success brought him further requests related to his mechanical and engineering expertise, such as improvements for a lamp used to light a fortress. Around 1593, Galileo invented a device to measure heat called a thermoscope, which functioned as an early version of a thermometer. Another invention was

Mathematics, Mechanics, and Motion

Galileo's thermoscope provided a means of quantifying the intensity of heat. Galileo found as the temperature changes, the water rises or falls in the glass neck in proportion to its density.

35

THE GEOMETRIC AND MILITARY COMPASS

One of Galileo's early successes was the invention of an instrument called a "geometric and military compass." It was based on a sector, which could

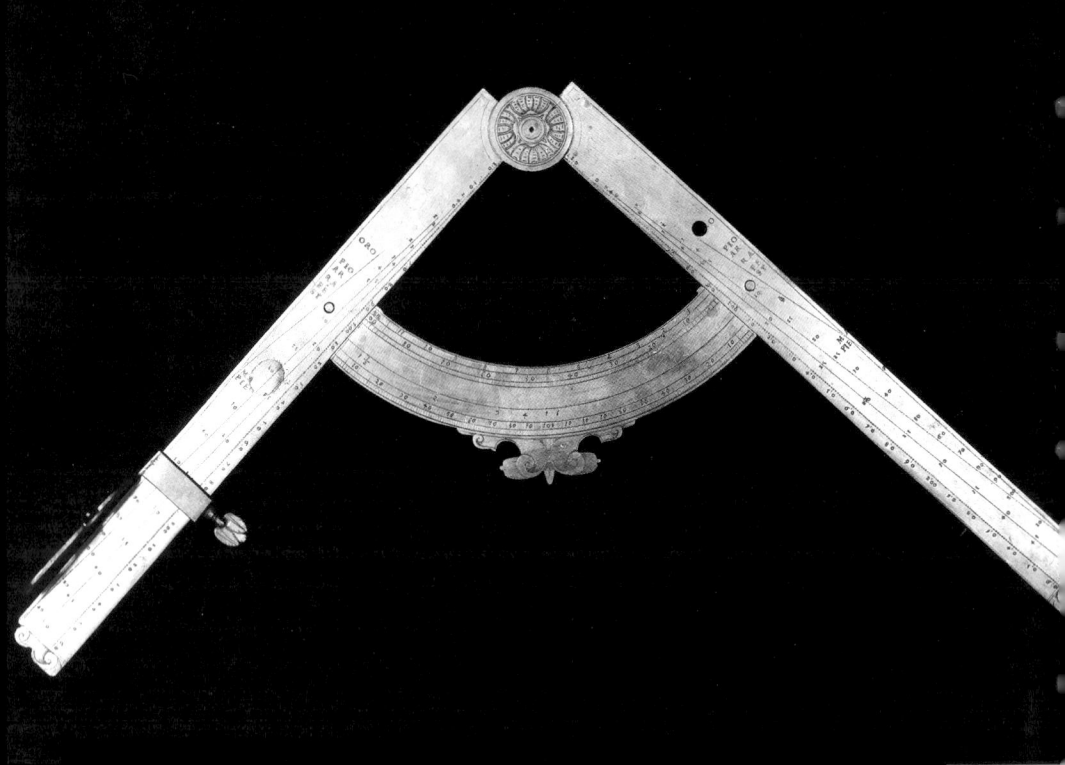

Galileo's geometric and military compass enabled military gunners and surveyors to calculate distances more quickly and accurately than with similar instruments of the time.

be used to gauge distances. It looked similar to two rulers that were connected by a pivot and that moved over a curved crosspiece called a quadrant. Galileo's instrument enabled cannoneers aiming a cannon to determine the height and distance of their target as well as the appropriate angle of elevation for the cannon's barrel. It could also be adapted for surveying. Galileo designed the instrument and set up a partnership with an artisan who produced the compass—the man and his family lodged in Galileo's home for many years. Galileo earned money selling the instrument, but he made even more by offering lessons in its use.

Galileo also produced an instruction manual for the geometric and military compass. In 1607, a man named Baldassare Capra plagiarized Galileo's manual, hinting that Galileo himself was the plagiarist. Galileo took him to court. He easily proved his claim that he had devised the instrument and written the manual. In court, he demonstrated that Capra didn't even fully understand how to use the compass.

an irrigation system that used the principles of Archimedes to extract water from an aquifer. He devised a geometric and military compass in 1597, which brought in a little money.

Galileo continued his physics research on the nature of moving bodies in Padua. He changed his focus from falling objects to objects moving down inclined planes, in which motion could be measured more accurately. He examined the velocity and trajectory of moving spheres as well as the timing of pendulums and the paths of projectiles. The very process of experimentation was groundbreaking in his time, as was his mathematical analysis of his findings. Despite his extensive experiments, Galileo did not publish his results until much later in his life.

CHAPTER THREE

Peering Through the Telescope

Despite the productive research and notable accomplishments of his years at the University of Padua, Galileo began to chafe at the requirements of his teaching job. More than the inadequate salary, Galileo resented the time dedicated to delivering dry lectures that he would rather have spent in other pursuits.

Between his professional and social life, Galileo kept busy. He frequently traveled to nearby Venice for entertainment and company. One of his closest friends, Gianfrancesco Sagredo, was a nobleman who lived in an opulent Venetian palace.

Galileo also established a relationship with Marina Gamba, a woman he met in Venice. She was fourteen years younger than him and came from an impoverished family. Marina became pregnant, and

Galileo's cathedra, or chair, is located in the Great Hall of the Palazzo Bo at the University of Padua. Galileo lectured from this chair at the internationally prestigious university, which was established in 1222.

Galileo moved her to lodgings close to his own house in Padua. She had three children with him, who he named after his sisters and father—Virginia in 1600, Livia in 1601, and Vincenzo in 1606. Galileo was not listed as their father on their birth certificates, and he and Marina never married.

He continued to experience financial difficulties related to supporting his growing family. In addition to supplying dowries for both of his sisters, he was paying to help his brother establish a living as a musician. When Galileo renewed his contract with the University of Padua in 1599, his friend Sagredo helped negotiate a raise to 320 florins a year.

A "NEW STAR"

Galileo's interest in astronomy began during his early years teaching at the University of Padua. His first known speculation on the subject dates from 1595, when he sought to explain ocean tides. He theorized that the tides rose and fell because of the movement of the earth. His explanation was incorrect, but it did demonstrate that Galileo was receptive to the notion that the earth could move. This idea contradicted the Aristotelian assumption of the stationary earth being at the center of the universe.

Also in 1595, Galileo began corresponding with the esteemed astronomer Johannes Kepler, who published a book in 1596 called *Mysterium Cosmographicum* (Cosmographic Mystery, also published as *The Secret of*

Galileo Galilei

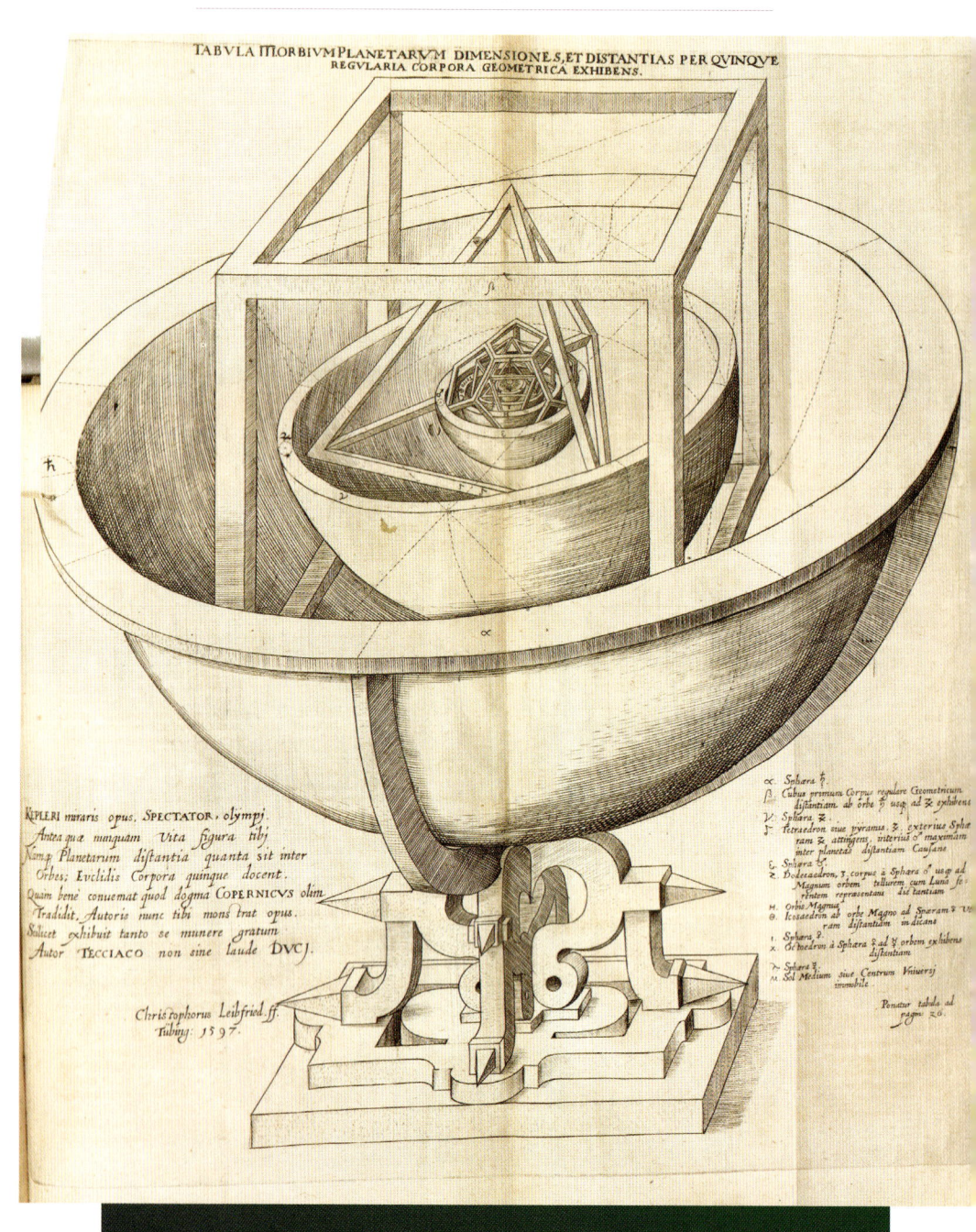

A picture from *Mysterium Cosmographicum* illustrates Kepler's model of the universe, in which the nesting spheres represent the orbits of the planets.

the Universe) that assumed that the sun was the center of the universe. In 1597, Galileo wrote a letter to Kepler stating that he had agreed with Copernicanism for a long time and even had written a defense of the theory, which no longer exists. Still, he had continued teaching the Aristotelian system of the universe at the University of Padua. He did not want to risk publicly defending Copernicanism when charges of heresy against church teachings could bring serious consequences. In addition, at this time, proponents of Copernicanism could provide little evidence supporting the heliocentric model.

In 1604, scientific circles and the public alike were captivated by the emergence of a "new star" in the sky that was brighter than any of the other stars or planets. Over the next eighteen months, its light gradually faded. Today, scientists know that the new star was a supernova, the result of a star exploding cataclysmically. In Galileo's day, the event held great philosophical, astronomical, theological, and astrological significance. People believed that such an extraordinary spectacle could be an omen of impending disasters. The church feared the phenomenon because it contradicted the belief that the heavens were fixed into place.

The leading astronomers across Europe were called upon to explain the event, which is now called "Kepler's nova" because Kepler was credited with its discovery. Galileo gave three lectures on the new star in Padua. Scientists of his day did not have the instruments or knowledge to explain the nature of the phenomenon. They could, however, give an opinion on how near the star was to the earth. Galileo and other astronomers observed the star's movement over time. They found that its position remained fixed relative to the other stars in the sky, unlike the planets and moon. Therefore, the star was located in the heavens beyond the moon, not in the earthly realm.

This conclusion put Galileo at odds with strict Aristotelian scholars. According to the Aristotelian model, the objects in the heavens were composed of an unchanging material called quintessence, a pure, perfect substance. Aristotle's cosmology could not account for a new object appearing in the heavens. Following his lectures, Galileo engaged in a prolonged public duel with a colleague, a supporter of Aristotelianism named Cesare Cremonini. It is possible that the "new star" caused Galileo to speculate that the earth was moving in relation to the stars, not the other way around as described by the Aristotelian model.

PEERING THROUGH THE TELESCOPE

DEVELOPMENT OF THE TELESCOPE

In 1609, Galileo heard a description of a novel optical instrument, invented in the Netherlands, that made faraway objects appear three times closer than their

At the top of the Tower of St. Mark's in Venice, Galileo demonstrates his telescope before Doge Leonardo Dona and a group of advisers, who were astonished by the instrument's capabilities.

actual distance. This marvel was an early version of the telescope. Soon, scholars across Europe were excitedly discussing the new device.

Galileo received the news during a period of personal and professional dissatisfaction. He was feeling weighed down by his responsibilities to his family and frustrated with his duties at the university. None of his inventions had made his fortune, as he'd hoped, and he was still searching for a breakthrough project that would bring recognition and financial security. His dream was to return to Florence and serve in the court of the Medicis.

Galileo's friend Sarpi had read a description of the new instrument and dismissed it as uninteresting. But Galileo realized that the device could have significant military value, and the instrument had not yet been formally presented in Venice. Galileo rushed to his workshop. Based on the description of a tube containing two lenses, he easily recreated the instrument through trial and error using various lenses—he did not fully understand the optical principles at work. By his own account, he managed to produce a working telescope within a period of twenty-four hours.

Next, Galileo set to work on improving the instrument. He quickly succeeded in constructing a nine-power telescope of a much higher quality than the versions that had previously been demonstrated.

In August 1609, Galileo formally displayed his telescope to the chief magistrate of Venice—the doge—

Two of Galileo's early telescopes are seen here. After constructing his first telescope, Galileo quickly improved the instrument by making it more powerful, which he achieved by grinding larger, more precise lenses.

and some of the most important figures in Venice, including the commanders of the Venetian navy. They examined the instrument and ascended the Tower of Saint Mark's, the highest point in the city. Looking through the telescope, they could view buildings in distant Padua and watch people entering a church on a neighboring island. The demonstration was a triumph.

A few days later, Galileo presented the telescope to the doge as a gift. As a reward, Galileo's salary was doubled and his professorship guaranteed for life.

Galileo got to work constructing telescopes. He succeeded in increasing the strength and incorporated other improvements. For many years, his telescopes were the finest available.

THE STARRY MESSENGER

Although Galileo had emphasized the telescope's potential for military applications to the doge, he also recognized the promise it held for science. He knew that his fellow scientists would put the telescope to use for research, as well. If he wanted to make new discoveries about the nature of the heavens, he would have to work quickly.

In the winter of 1609, Galileo turned his telescope to the sky. He used his most powerful telescope, which enlarged objects twenty times. Galileo began by observing the moon. Through the telescope, he could

Galileo included drawings of the phases of the moon in his *Sidereus Nuncius* that depicted features of the lunar surface such as craters and mountains.

recognize surface features such as mountains and craters, which he recorded in drawings.

During a trip to Florence, Galileo paid a visit to Cosimo de' Medici, known as Cosimo II, the grand duke of Tuscany, and showed him the view of the moon through the telescope. Galileo was already well acquainted with the grand duke because he had tutored him in mathematics as a boy. Cosimo was amazed by the sight of the moon and rewarded Galileo with 800 crowns. Galileo departed with hope that the grand duke would offer him a position in Tuscany.

Turning his telescope to the open sky, he observed that many stars existed that could not be detected with the naked eye. He realized that the Milky Way was composed of stars. Galileo's early observations were already contradicting the Aristotelian model. According to Aristotle, the moon's face was smooth and the Milky Way was made up of an exhalation emitted by stars.

On January 7, 1610, Galileo observed Jupiter for the first time. He noticed an interesting alignment of three stars alongside the planet—two to the east and one to the west. Astonishingly, when he peered at Jupiter the next night, their positions had changed. All three appeared to the west of the planet. Two nights after that, only two of the three were visible, this time to the east of Jupiter. The next night brought another surprise. Four "stars" surrounded Jupiter—three to the west and one to the east. Galileo's first theory was that the little stars were

KEPLER'S ENDORSEMENT

Galileo released *The Starry Messenger* to great acclaim and some disbelief. Early support came from Johannes Kepler.

Kepler had worked briefly as an assistant to the great astronomer Tycho Brahe, who revolutionized astronomical instruments and observation practices. Brahe also developed the Tychonic model of the universe, in which the sun and moon revolved around a stationary earth, but the other planets orbited the sun. Kepler, however, subscribed to Copernicanism. Kepler succeeded Brahe as imperial mathematician, the most prestigious mathematics post in Europe. His own outstanding contribution to astronomy was the development of the laws of planetary motion.

After reading *The Starry Messenger*, Kepler published a strong defense of Galileo's claims about the moons of Jupiter even before he had a chance to observe them himself. He recognized that the existence of the Galilean moons supported his interpretation of Copernicanism.

traveling across the sky in the vicinity of Jupiter. But then he came to the correct conclusion that the four celestial objects were actually moons that were orbiting Jupiter.

Galileo realized that he had made a momentous discovery, and he resolved to publish his findings quickly. Over the next couple of months, he rushed to record his observations and conclusions. He gave his work the title *Sidereus Nuncius (The Sidereal Messenger* or *The Starry Messenger)*, in which Galileo himself was the messenger bringing a report from the stars. The book included precisely rendered illustrations of the moon. In most of his later works, Galileo would not bother creating such high-quality illustrations because he assumed that readers had access to telescopes and would be able to make their own observations.

In the text of the book, Galileo took advantage of another opportunity to gain favor with the grand duke of Tuscany. He gave Jupiter's four moons the title, "the Medicean stars."

The book was released on March 12, 1610. *The Starry Messenger* was met with widespread excitement across Europe even though it was intended for an intellectual readership and written in Latin. All 550 copies of the first edition sold out within a week. Across Europe, people tried to obtain telescopes so that they could view the marvels for themselves. Galileo sent his finest telescopes to high-ranking aristocrats.

Galileo drew on his newfound fame to urge Cosimo to grant him a position in the Tuscan court. In a letter to his brother-in-law, Galileo had bemoaned being "held for life" in Venice despite his fantastic success. Galileo visited

Florence over Easter and showed Cosimo the moons of Jupiter through a telescope. He also discussed terms of employment with the grand duke's secretary of state. Galileo wanted the grand duke to match his salary at Venice, and he asked for two years paid in advance. He did not want to be required to lecture or hold any other public duties. Galileo also presented a long list of topics that he planned to research and write on.

Sagredo and other friends in Venice, however, urged him to reconsider leaving. They pointed out that Venice was a republic, and it would protect him from possible consequences of condemnation by the Catholic Church. In Florence, by contrast, his life, livelihood, and security would be in the hands of a single nobleman. Furthermore, if the sickly Cosimo died, his successor might not hold Galileo in such high favor.

Nonetheless, in July, Cosimo made Galileo an offer that granted all of his terms. Galileo would be the chief mathematician at the University of Pisa, and mathematician and philosopher of the Tuscan court. Galileo had particularly requested the title of "philosopher," a position generally considered higher status than a mere mathematician. He arrived in Florence in September, never to return to Venice.

CHAPTER FOUR

COPERNICANISM AND CONTROVERSY

Galileo returned to his observations with the telescope soon after taking up his new post in Florence. Upon viewing Saturn, it became apparent that the planet was usually seen in direct proximity to two smaller celestial bodies that Galileo described as Saturn's "ears." Astronomers of his day could not explain the phenomenon. Decades later, it was recognized that Saturn was encircled by rings. (Today, astronomers know that the rings are made of ice and rock.)

Observations of Venus also revealed properties that could not be detected by the naked eye. Galileo noted that Venus had phases, like the earth's moon. Both the traditional geocentric model as well as Copernicus's heliocentric model predicted the phases of Venus. Tracking the changing phases could determine whether Venus

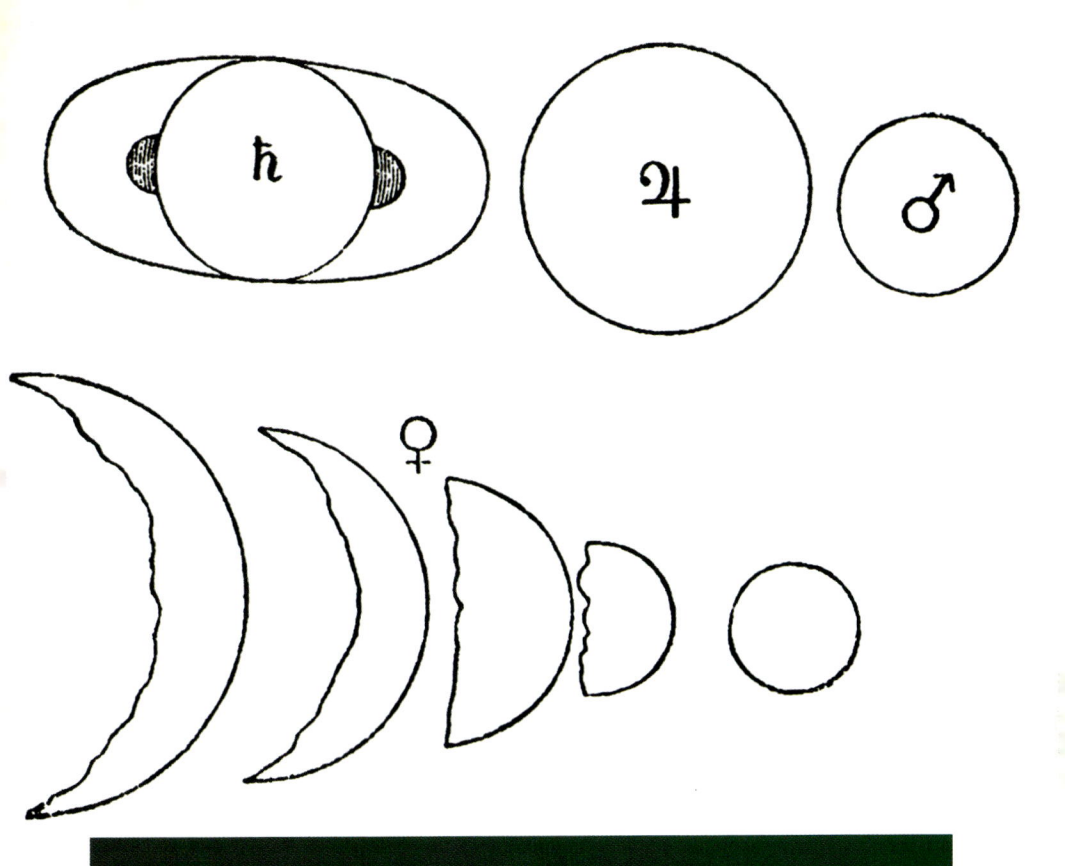

Galileo's observations of the planets revealed new unexpected features, such as the phases of Venus (*bottom*) and the "ears" (now known as rings) of Saturn (*top left*) that he recorded in drawings.

was orbiting the earth or the sun. In December, Venus appeared as a half-planet, which was possible only in the Copernican model. However, Galileo was not yet ready to publicly endorse Copernicanism.

Galileo also aimed his telescope at the sun, making observations through clouds at sunset. He discerned the existence of sunspots that appeared and faded on the face of the sun. Only after long-term observation would Galileo reach conclusions about the nature of sunspots and what they revealed about the sun.

In 1611, Galileo traveled to Rome to demonstrate his discoveries to the officials of the Catholic Church. He renewed his acquaintance with Clavius, who had also been observing Jupiter's moons with a telescope. Pope Paul V granted him an audience. The pope's principal adviser, Cardinal Robert Bellarmine, questioned the Roman College—a Jesuit institution of learning—about the validity of Galileo's claims. The scholars confirmed Galileo's observations of Jupiter's moons and the phases of Venus, the two points with the most significance to church doctrine. Galileo was treated like a celebrity during his visit to Rome, and he made many important contacts during formal and social gatherings.

His position in the Tuscan court granted Galileo financial security and an end to the money troubles related to his family responsibilities. His two daughters had moved to Florence, as well, and they entered a convent. Marina Gamba and Galileo's young son, Vincenzo, remained in Padua. Health issues began to affect the quality of his life, however. As early as 1604, Galileo had begun to suffer from rheumatism. Later, he experienced periodic attacks of fever, insomnia, loss of blood, and various pains that could render him bedridden for weeks or months. He also complained about fits of severe melancholy, which today might be diagnosed as anxiety or depression. During his trip to Rome, Galileo's carriage had to be outfitted specially with a bed because of his ill health.

Robert Bellarmine, an Italian Jesuit and a cardinal and defender of the Catholic Church, was often involved in deciding theological controversies, including the validity of Copernicanism.

INVESTIGATION OF FLOATING BODIES

Galileo's breakthroughs had been well received by the Catholic Church. So far, he had avoided the controversy and censure provoked by some scientists and philosophers introducing new ideas and discoveries. Nevertheless, *The Starry Messenger* received its share of criticism upon its release. At first, some viewers using the early, blurry telescopes had difficulty discerning the moons of Jupiter. Even after their existence was accepted, some people still held doubts that they could trust the reality of the images seen through the telescope.

People paid little attention to a few significant passages in the work—three places in which Galileo endorses Copernicanism. Following the apparent public acceptance of ideas that contradicted the established model, Galileo went on to challenge another aspect of Aristotelianism.

Soon after returning to Florence, Galileo became involved in an intellectual dispute over the nature of ice. He had become close friends with a young man named Fillippo Salviati, a former student, and Galileo spent much time at Salviati's palace. A visiting professor from Pisa stated that ice consisted of condensed water that was heavier than liquid water. It floated because of its flat shape. Drawing on the principles of Archimedes, Galileo retorted that ice was lighter than water. An object's density determined whether or not it would float regardless of its shape.

One of Galileo's rivals at the University of Pisa joined the debate. Lodovico delle Colombe was the most prominent member of the so-called pigeon league of staunch Aristotelian proponents—his name is similar to the word for "pigeon." Colombe demonstrated the apparent truth of the Aristotelian position by placing a chip of ebony and a sphere of ebony in water. The chip floated, but the sphere sank. Galileo challenged Colombe to a contest over the issue, and all of the intellectuals of Florence excitedly awaited the showdown.

The grand duke, however, forbade Galileo to engage in the public face-off. He told Galileo that he should make his case in writing instead.

The result was Galileo's second significant work on physics, a treatise published in 1612 as *Discorso intorno alle cose, che stanno in sù l'acqua, ò che in quella si muovono* (generally known as *Discourse on Floating Bodies* or *Discourse on Bodies in Water*). This work was written in Italian, as were all of his subsequent works. It was, therefore, more accessible to the general public. Specifically, it was written in Tuscan Italian, which differed from the Italian of Rome and other parts of modern-day Italy.

In *Discourse on Floating Bodies*, Galileo explained the floating chip of ebony by claiming that it was buoyed by an air pocket. (He was incorrect—today, people know that the reason is the surface tension of water.) Galileo described experiments involving various

Galileo Galilei

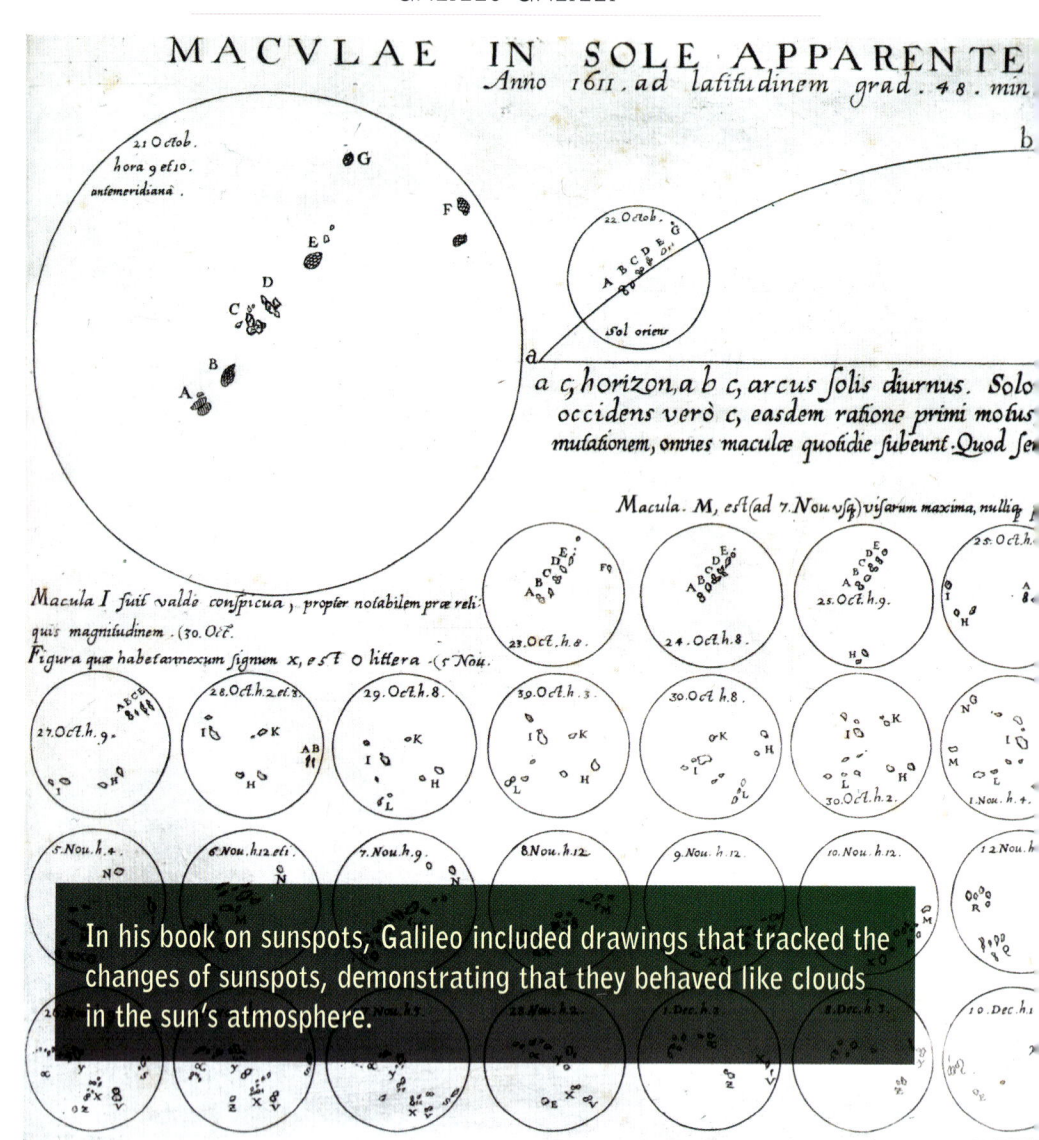

MACVLAE IN SOLE APPARENTE
Anno 1611. ad latitudinem grad. 48. min.

In his book on sunspots, Galileo included drawings that tracked the changes of sunspots, demonstrating that they behaved like clouds in the sun's atmosphere.

bodies' behaviors in water and used mathematics to support his position. Controversially, he rejected Aristotle's notion that some objects by their essential nature had a tendency to rise while others tended to fall. Instead, he focused on density, a measurable physical property.

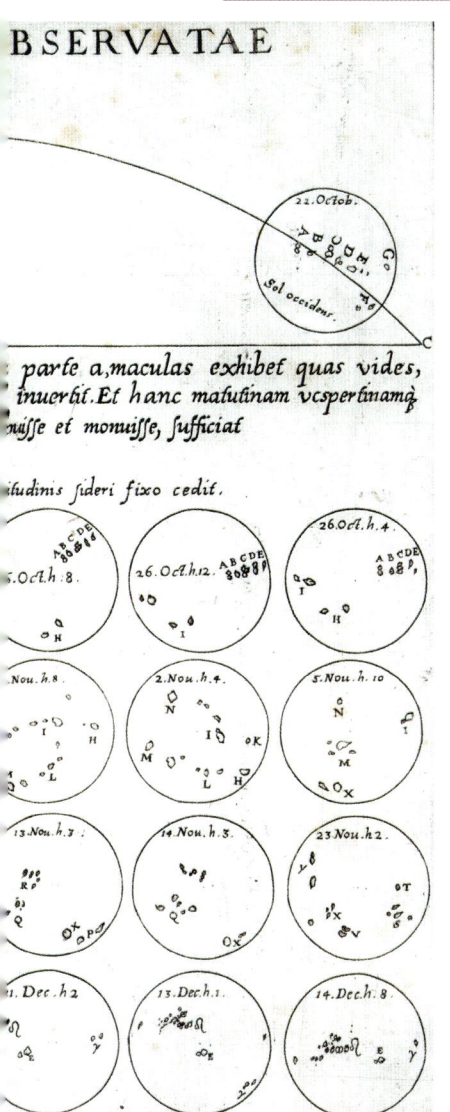

The work attracted public interest, and two editions sold out. Four books written by other philosophers attacked the views on Aristotelianism that Galileo expressed in *Discourse on Floating Bodies*.

CONTENTIOUS LETTERS

Galileo had become an expert in performing astronomic observations. One of his techniques allowed him to observe the sun indirectly by projecting its image onto a sheet of paper. He made extensive observations of the sun, tracking sunspots as they arose and subsided. But in 1612, he was alarmed to hear that another scholar going by the pseudonym of Apelles claimed to have discovered sunspots before Galileo.

Apelles asserted that sunspots were small planet-like bodies that passed between the earth and the sun. This theory upheld the Aristotelian model of the earth being at the center of the universe. Galileo concluded that sunspots were a phenomenon of the sun's atmosphere—another repudiation of the Aristotelian view that heavenly bodies were perfect and unchanging. By tracking the movement of individual sunspots, Galileo discovered that the sun was rotating on an axis. Galileo wrote three letters reporting his observations and refuting the claims of Apelles, who was found to be Christoph Scheiner, a German Jesuit astronomer. The dispute caused Scheiner to become Galileo's lifelong enemy.

Istoria e dimostrazioni intorno alle macchie solari e loro accidenti (History and demonstrations concerning sunspots and their properties) was published in 1613. It included the three letters as well as an appendix, in which Galileo reported that he had devised a means of anticipating the eclipses of Jupiter's satellites. He considered this to be scientific confirmation of Copernicanism, because the calculations took into account the changes in the earth's position relative to Jupiter. Surely other scholars would recognize that the Aristotelian system was erroneous.

Also in 1613, Galileo was drawn into the debate over Copernicanism with Benedetto Castelli, his friend and former student. Castelli was a Benedictine monk who had come to Florence to assist his former teacher in his scientific work. One evening, during dinner with the grand duke, Cosimo's mother, Grand Duchess Christina, questioned Castelli about Copernicanism. She pointed out certain passages in the Bible that contradicted the

The powerful Grand Duchess Christina, mother of Cosimo de' Medici, sparked Galileo's defense of Copernicanism when she questioned whether the theory contradicted the Bible.

theory that the earth was moving around the sun. Galileo responded with his *Letter to Castelli*, in which he put forth arguments reconciling Copernicanism and scientific observations with biblical teachings. Copies of the letter were distributed among scholars, and it was read by his enemies as well as his friends.

Some historians consider Galileo's *Letter to Castelli* the biggest mistake he made during his entire life. The wider world was not yet ready to accept Copernicanism, or its implications that the earth was moving under people's feet, the moon was a gargantuan boulder in the sky, and the heavens were unstable. Most significant, factions within the Catholic Church objected to Galileo's ideas, which challenged religious dogma as well as the Aristotelian worldview.

In 1614, Tommaso Caccini, a Dominican friar who had attacked Galileo in the past, denounced Copernicanism, declaring it heretical. This time, however, the charges reached the Inquisition, which obtained a copy of the *Letter to Castelli*. The investigation sparked debate over Copernicanism, which had both supporters and opponents within the Catholic Church. Cardinal Robert Bellarmine, who had condemned Bruno to death, held the view that Copernicus's work should be used only for theoretical calculations, not to explain the real world.

Galileo decided to travel to Rome to defend Copernicanism. Ahead of his visit, he expanded his thoughts on Copernicanism and church doctrine in the

> ## THE INQUISITION
>
> The Inquisition was the Catholic Church's judicial institution charged with suppressing heresy. Galileo was tried by the Roman Inquisition, which was set up in the mid-sixteenth century. It consisted of a panel of cardinals advised by theological scholars who served as consultants.
>
> The Inquisition held considerable power and operated in fearsome secrecy. The subjects of their investigation were not told the identity of their accusers or even the charges being brought against them. If the Inquisition was convinced that the accused was guilty, torture could be used to coerce a confession. Possible sentences included a penitential pilgrimage, confinement in a monastery, or, in the most extreme cases, capital punishment.

1615 *Letter to the Grand Duchess Christina*. He took this step despite warnings from his friends to leave discussion of religious doctrine to theologians. Like the *Letter to Castelli*, it was intended for circulation among scholars. The *Letter to the Grand Duchess Christina*—actually a forty-page manuscript in which Galileo declares his allegiance to Copernicanism—was not published openly until many years later.

A WARNING FROM THE INQUISITION

Galileo's friends and supporters were apprehensive about his upcoming arrival in Rome. For one thing, his presence would make little difference in the ongoing investigation by the Catholic Church. The matter had mostly been decided. Although Bellarmine did not subscribe to Copernicanism as a theologian, he did not advocate a ban on Copernican theory. Galileo's letters had been deemed, for the most part, free of heresies—and he had the protection of the grand duke of Tuscany.

However, as the Tuscan ambassador warned Cosimo, it was not an opportune time to introduce new ideas in Rome. Pope Paul V had a reputation for being anti-intellectual. He also wanted to prevent disputes between different religious orders within the church. It was possible that he could suppress a matter of theological debate to preserve cooperation. If Galileo advocated too stridently for Copernicanism, it could hurt his cause.

Galileo arrived in Rome on December 10, 1615. He was confident that he would succeed in winning people over to the truth of his new scientific vision. Disregarding warnings from his friends that he should avoid drawing too much attention to himself, Galileo circulated from one audience to another promoting Copernicanism. He won his arguments, but he failed to win over doubters. Bellarmine and other important figures refused to meet with him.

Copernicanism and Controversy

The matter of Copernicanism was under discussion by a group of theologians called Qualifiers. They were disquieted by Galileo's showmanship, and they viewed it as an attack on religious doctrine. On February 24, 1616, the panel announced their decision on two Copernican propositions: that the sun is the center of the universe and does not move, and that the earth is not the center of the universe and does move. The Qualifiers ruled both of these controversial concepts to be heretical and erroneous according to their interpretation of Holy Scripture. The cardinals that made up the Inquisition accepted the finding, and the pope directed Bellarmine to warn Galileo that he must abandon Copernicanism. Some books endorsing Copernicanism were banned. Copernicus's own works, however, were only suspended until certain passages could be censored, and none of Galileo's writings were banned.

On March 3, Bellarmine announced that he had issued the warning. However, the precise details of the February 26 meeting remain a historical mystery. Bellarmine had the option of giving Galileo a private informal warning or a formal warning before witnesses. It is known that he notified Galileo of the Qualifiers' decision on Copernicanism. But did he also issue the stronger, formal warning? In 1633, a document was found in Galileo's file that was kept by the Inquisition stating that he had been read a strongly worded text prohibiting him from holding, defending, or teaching Copernicanism in any way. This formal warning was not signed or notarized, however, and neither Bellarmine nor a witness who was present at the exchange was still alive in 1633.

After the proceedings, speculation persisted that Galileo had been convicted of heresy and punished. At his request, on May 26, Bellarmine issued Galileo a certificate to dispel such rumors. It stated that Galileo had been informed of the Catholic Church's ruling on Copernicanism and it did not mention any formal warning.

CHAPTER FIVE

The *Dialogue* and Condemnation

Galileo gradually began to withdraw from social and court life. He tasked Castelli with teaching the grand duke's son Ferdinando and neglected some of his correspondence. His health deteriorated. He now suffered from arthritis and a hernia, as well as from his other chronic ailments. Beginning in 1617, Galileo spent much of his time in a villa outside Florence. He tended the grounds and paid frequent visits to his daughters, who lived in a nearby convent. Both took new names upon joining the order. Virginia became Maria Celeste. Livia, who chose the name Arcangela, grew depressed under the harsh conditions of the convent. Their mother, Marina Gamba, had died in 1612. Cosimo eventually legitimized Galileo's son, Vincenzo, which granted him some legal rights. Galileo's own mother, Giulia, died in 1620.

Ottavio Leoni drew this portrait of Galileo in 1624. In the years immediately following his warning from the Inquisition, Galileo's physical health faltered and he was too ill to make astronomical observations.

The grand duke died in 1621, leaving his ten-year-old son, Ferdinando, as his heir. His mother and grandmother served as regents until the boy reached the age of eighteen. Like his father, Ferdinando was Galileo's friend and supporter.

THE NATURE OF SCIENCE

Although forbidden to address Copernicanism, Galileo turned to other areas of research. He invented a device that determined longitude by observing the moons of Jupiter and unsuccessfully tried to sell it. He had returned to his writings on motion when he was sidetracked by the appearance of three comets in 1618.

Dispute about the nature of the comets led him to release his next book, *Il saggiatore* (*The Assayer*). An "assayer" is a highly precise balance used to weigh gold and other precious metals. The volume served as a rebuttal to Grassi's book *Astronomical and Physical Balance*, arguing against his claims concerning comets as well as broader subjects, including methods of scientific reasoning. Galileo's theory about comets was incorrect—he held that they were distortions of light in the atmosphere. Nonetheless, *The Assayer* is remembered as Galileo's manifesto on the nature of science and how humans view reality. He defended mathematics as a means of understanding the world. He also differentiated between primary qualities, such as an object's size and shape, as

THE COMET DEBATES

Between August and November 1618, three comets were observed in the sky, the third remarkably vivid. Many people wondered what omen they signified, but astronomers were more interested in their scientific characteristics. Were these bodies situated in the heavens or, as Aristotle believed, in the earthly realm? In 1619, a Jesuit astronomer named Orazio

The Great Comet of 1618, shown here over Heidelberg, Germany, was the last of three comets occurring in rapid succession that led to debate among scientists and fear of coming doom among ordinary people.

The *Dialogue* and Condemnation

Grassi released a pamphlet called *De Tribus Cometis Anni MDCXVIII Disputatio Astonomica* (*An Astronomical Discussion of the Three Comets of 1618*), in which he asserted that the comet was located in the heavens. He published it anonymously, although the author's identity was well known.

Galileo decided to issue a rebuttal to Grassi's work, even though he had been too ill to observe the comets himself. He did not issue his rebuttal under his own name, though. Instead, a pupil of Galileo's, Mario Guiducci, released *Discorso delle comete* (*Discourse on the Comets*). Everyone in Galileo's circle knew that the pamphlet held Galileo's own thoughts on the subject. Surprisingly, it claimed that comets were a phenomenon in the earthly realm.

Grassi struck back with a book called *Libra Astronomica ac Philosophica* (*The Astronomical and Philosophical Balance*), written under a different pseudonym. Galileo responded with *Il saggiatore* (*The Assayer*), now considered one of his significant works, using his own name. The debate over comets ended with Grassi's 1626 work, *Ratio Ponderum Librae et Simbellae* (A Reckoning of Weights for the Balance and the Small Scale), but resentment lingered over the attacks launched during the war of words.

opposed to secondary qualities, such as odors and colors, which he described as sensations existing only in the observer's consciousness. Galileo speculated that some such phenomenon, such as heat, could be explained by the motion of tiny particles. This train of thought anticipated ideas that would be debated by future philosophers and scientists.

The tone of *The Assayer* was witty and sarcastic, and the book made Grassi into Galileo's enemy. It also alienated the Jesuit order, which had not been altogether hostile to Galileo before that point.

In 1623, Maffeo Barberini took office as Pope Urban VIII. Barberini had been a supporter of Galileo who took an interest in his scientific work. Galileo hoped that the new pope would bring a more open-minded attitude toward Copernicanism and scientific innovations. *The Assayer* was nearly ready to be published, and Galileo added an extravagant dedication to Pope Urban VIII. Galileo was delighted to hear that the pope read and appreciated the book.

The next year, Galileo traveled to Rome to meet with the pope. He received a warm reception, but Urban VIII gave no indication that he was planning to lift the ban on Copernicanism. Nonetheless, Galileo left with the understanding that he could write about Copernicanism as long as he treated the arguments as hypothetical.

Pope Urban VIII, who formerly had been supportive of Galileo, grew increasingly paranoid, tyrannical, and intolerant of any hint of criticism after he took office as pope.

GALILEO'S *DIALOGUE*

Galileo spent the next six years working on the book that would be published under the title *Dialogo sopra i due massimi sistemi del mondo, Tolemaico e Copernicano* (*Dialogue Concerning the Two Chief World Systems, Ptolemaic and Copernican*, often referred to simply as the *Dialogue*). The work stood as his defense of Copernicanism, although it abided by the requirement that the model be presented as theoretical. Galileo initially gave it the title "Dialogue on the Ebb and Flow of the Sea." It was dedicated to Ferdinando, the grand duke of Tuscany.

The *Dialogue* takes the form of a conversation among three people, two of whom are philosophers. The Aristotelian philosopher is called Simplicio. Galileo named the other two characters in tribute to two of his dearest friends, both of whom had died. The Copernican philosopher is named Salviati. The third character is named Sagredo, a man who is imaginative and intelligent although he is not trained in philosophy.

The book's structure consists of four days of conversation. The first day addresses Aristotle's physics, focusing mainly on astronomy. Galileo points out the many discoveries that demonstrate that the heavens are changeable, contrary to the Aristotelian model. The second day deals with the rotation of the earth and the question of why, if the earth is moving, people cannot detect the motion. Galileo argued that motion is relative, and that people cannot detect the motion because they are moving at the same speed as the earth. The third day addresses the notion that the earth and other planets orbit the sun. As on the first day, Galileo uses his astronomical observations to bolster his arguments. The fourth day discusses the tides, and Galileo puts forth his theory that is now known to be erroneous.

Family issues and health problems had slowed Galileo's progress on the *Dialogue* during the late 1620s. Galileo was developing cataracts, which would eventually lead to blindness. Finally, he announced the completion of the book in early 1630 and began sharing passages with his friends. In May, he traveled to Rome to make arrangements about publishing the *Dialogue*. He met with several important officials in the Catholic Church, the most important being Pope Urban VIII himself. The pope made no objections to the content of the *Dialogue*, although he directed that Galileo change the title. It would not be appropriate to imply that this theoretical work explained the tides, a real physical phenomenon.

Circumstances delayed release of the *Dialogue*. Francesco Cesi, Galileo's friend and patron who had planned to publish the book, died suddenly. Plague had struck Italy. Official approval by the Catholic Church was delayed, and Galileo began to grow concerned. His friend Castelli sent him a letter advising him to publish the *Dialogue* in Florence instead of Rome, and as quickly as possible. Finally, in mid-1631, the church censors approved the text, although they added a preface and conclusion that emphasized that Copernicanism was hypothetical.

The *Dialogue* was published in Florence in 1632. Initial reception was positive, although some of Galileo's old enemies raised objections. However, the pope had soured on the *Dialogue*. Galileo's onetime supporter had changed since taking power. He tended to be superstitious and paranoid, and he tolerated no perceived challenges to his authority. He had become convinced that Galileo had cast him in the role of Simplicio in the book.

The pope ordered that publication of the *Dialogue* be halted. The Tuscan ambassador met with the pope and found him exploding in rage at Galileo. In September, Pope Urban VIII sent the *Dialogue* to be examined by an official commission. The group referred the *Dialogue* to the Inquisition.

THE TRIAL

On October 1, Galileo was summoned to appear before the court of the Inquisition

The *Dialogue* and Condemnation

on charges of heresy. He asked to be given an exemption on the grounds of his poor health, but the pope would not allow it. Galileo arrived in Rome in February 1633.

A painting of his trial portrays Galileo (*kneeling at left*) symbolically pushing away the Bible. In reality, Galileo was devastated by the proceedings and showed no sign of resistance.

The proceedings against Galileo by the Inquisition lasted from April 12 until April 30. He was confined during this time, but he stayed in comfortable rooms, not a prison cell, and was attended by servants. He was not tortured during the interrogation although he may have been under threat of torture.

The document describing Bellarmine's prohibition on teaching Copernicanism was brought up as evidence. Galileo had certainly violated those terms in the *Dialogue*, even if he was treating it as hypothetical. Despite that, Galileo was able to produce the certificate he'd been given by Bellarmine that merely held him to the official ruling on Copernicanism.

During his first interrogation sessions, Galileo insisted that he had complied with the terms on the certificate, and he stated that he could not recall being ordered against holding, defending, or teaching Copernicanism "in any way." He even claimed that his book rejected Copernicanism. A couple of weeks later, the commissary of the Inquisition, Father Vincenzo Maculano, paid Galileo a visit for a private conversation. Three days later, another formal interrogation took place. This time, Galileo confessed that in his vanity, he had perhaps overstated some of his arguments concerning tides and sunspots. He even offered to add additional dialogues to the book to clarify his positions.

Galileo was allowed to go free. On May 10, he presented his formal defense before the Inquisition. He

The *Dialogue* and Condemnation

was hoping for a light sentence, and the Inquisition seemed to have been prepared to issue a token punishment. But there were objections made to lenient treatment of Galileo. It's not known who opposed Galileo, although some have guessed that it may have been the Jesuits or even the pope himself. Still, no official decision was made on his fate, and he was summoned for another formal interrogation on June 21. This time, under threat of torture, he was forced to recant Copernicanism.

On June 22, Galileo was declared guilty *de vehementi*—of vehement suspicion of heresy. The *Dialogue* was put on the church's list of banned books. Galileo was sentenced to indefinite imprisonment.

In July, Galileo departed Rome, never to return. But he was not thrown into a prison cell. Instead, he became an honored guest of Ascanio Piccolomini, the archbishop of Siena, a learned man who greatly admired Galileo. Piccolomini offered to host Galileo under house arrest.

Galileo was shattered and depressed after his ordeal. Piccolomini urged him to return to his scientific work and surrounded him with guests who could provide intellectual conversation. Galileo's health began to improve slightly, and he began to take up his writing on motion again.

By the end of the year, Galileo's sentence was reduced to house arrest in his own home. In December, he returned to Florence. Before his trial, Galileo had

Palazzo Piccolomini is located in Siena. Ascanio Piccolomini, the scholarly and wise archbishop of Siena, offered Galileo hospitality in the family's palace in the aftermath of Galileo's condemnation by the Inquisition.

moved to a smaller house near Florence, in Arcetri, close to his daughters' convent. For many years, Maria Celeste had been a great source of support and consolation. Much of her correspondence with her father still exists, and it shows that she was intelligent, compassionate, and pious. She helped tend his house during his absence. But Maria Celeste had long suffered from poor health herself because of the poverty and hardship she endured in the convent. She grew gravely ill in late 1633 and died in the spring of 1634. Galileo nearly gave way to despair following her death, and his health went into decline.

CHAPTER SIX

Two New Sciences and Galileo's Legacy

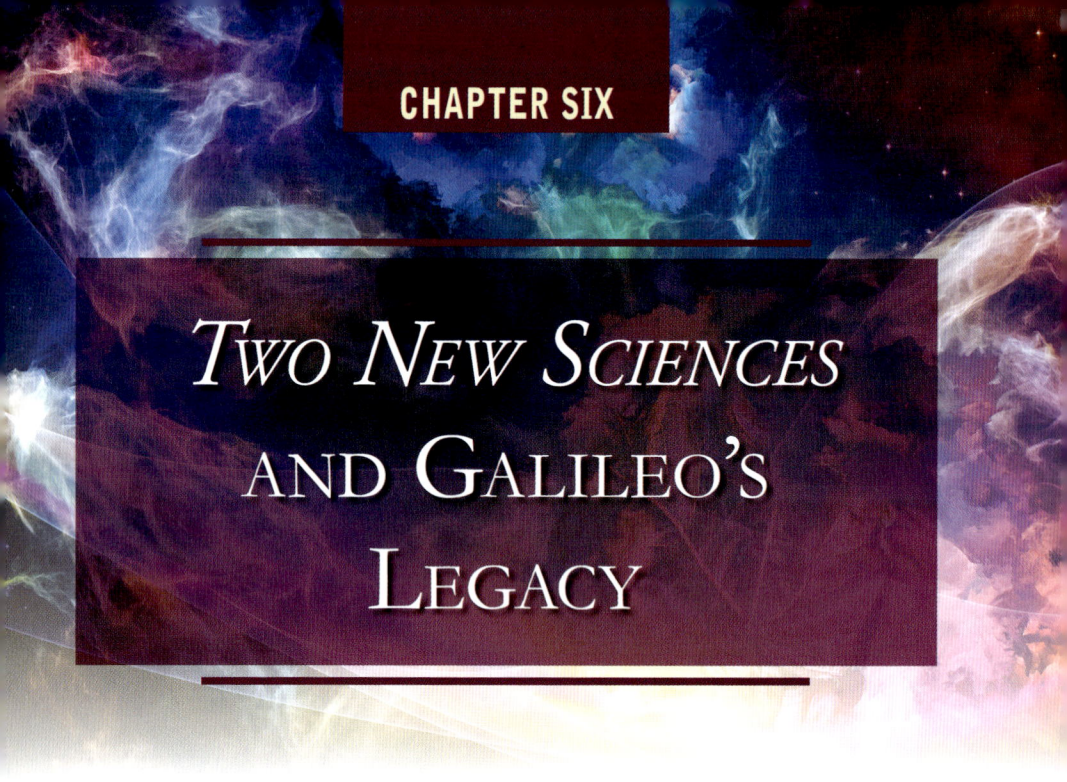

The terms of Galileo's confinement were strict, though enforcement became more flexible as time elapsed and Galileo became feebler. He could not have more than one or two visitors at a time. He rarely ventured farther from his home than the convent, although he occasionally received permission to travel. His correspondence was not restricted, but Galileo and his friends assumed that letters sent by mail might be read by church officials. Most of Galileo's circle of defenders continued to support him after the trial and sentencing—the grand duke did not waver—but they no longer knew who they could trust. Galileo's social and public standing was uncertain, and being Galileo's friend in these times could be a risky prospect.

Despite his difficult circumstances and poor health, Galileo was hard at work completing his treatise on physics and finding a publisher. He had decided to call his book "Dialogues on Motion." The church would not allow it to be published in Rome, nor in Venice. Finally, he found a publisher in the Netherlands, in the city of Leiden.

The manuscript was not immediately forthcoming, however. Galileo was losing his eyesight, and work was slow. Further, he knew that this was likely to be his last great achievement. He wanted to finalize and include all of his innovative ideas while there was still time.

INTRODUCING *TWO NEW SCIENCES*

The book was finally published in 1638 under the title *Discorsi e dimostrazioni matematiche intorno à due nuove scienze (Discourses and Mathematical Demonstrations Concerning Two New Sciences,* usually shortened to *Two New Sciences* or *Discourses*). It was dedicated to Count François de Noailles, the French ambassador to Rome, who helped facilitate publication. *Two New Sciences* is Galileo's contribution to physics, and it does not stray into Copernicanism or religion.

The two new sciences of the title are the examination of the nature of matter and of motion. As with *Dialogue,* the book takes the form of a conversation between Salviati, Sagredo, and Simplicio. This time, the

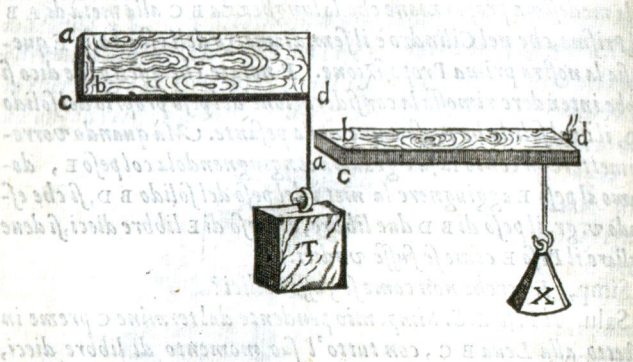

Galileo returned to mechanics and mathematics in his book *Two New Sciences*, two pages from which are shown here. The text includes discussion of the strength of rods and beams under different loads and placements.

Aristotelian Simplicio is wiser than in the earlier work. Once again, the book is divided into four days.

The action opens at the Venice Arsenal, where the

characters are amazed by the mechanical marvels. The first day introduces key concepts of Galileo's two new sciences. It also includes a discussion of pendulums and states a law of physics concerning the oscillation time of a pendulum. The second day focuses on the strength of different materials. The third day examines motion, and it presents some of Galileo's most important discoveries. His law of falling bodies, which examines the acceleration of objects as they fall, harks back to the days when he may have dropped objects off the top of the Leaning Tower of Pisa. The fourth day addresses the motion of projectiles and introduces another key discovery. Galileo demonstrates that the motion of a projectile has both horizontal and vertical components, and that a projectile's path is a curve called a parabola.

Two New Sciences was well received, and the Catholic Church took no action against Galileo following its publication. Galileo himself never read his own book, however. By late 1637, Galileo was totally blind.

Nonetheless, Galileo's intellect remained acute. Even as his vision dimmed in the summer of 1637, he made observations of the moon. He made the discovery that the moon rocked and wobbled slightly, allowing glimpses of slivers of the "far side." This phenomenon is called lunar libration.

Galileo was aided by two students who read out loud to him and attended to his correspondence. The Inquisition allowed them to live in his house. In a 1638 letter, he described his observation of lunar libration and even speculated that the movement of the moon could be related to the tides. In 1638, he briefly renewed his efforts to sell his invention for determining longitude at sea. Remembering his daughter's frustration with the unreliable clock at the convent, he discussed designs for a pendulum clock with his son, Vincenzo.

Galileo died in 1642 at the age of seventy-seven. His son and his two mathematical students were at his bedside.

AFTER GALILEO

Pope Urban VIII never abandoned his hostility to Galileo. Despite the extensive duties of his office, he reserved sole responsibility for the administrative task of licensing exemptions to read Galileo's *Dialogue*. Galileo bemoaned how the pope's zealotry would cause the book to be forgotten.

However, Galileo was wrong—even in the short-term, interest in his work remained keen. After the Catholic Church banned his *Dialogue*, Galileo worked to have the book translated into Latin and published abroad. His *Letter to the Grand Duchess Christina* was also released for the first time. In countries that were not dominated by the Catholic Church, the notion of a heliocentric solar system became widely accepted. During Galileo's last years, the philosopher Thomas Hobbes visited him and informed him that the *Dialogue* had been translated into English.

The pope also forbade Galileo's burial in consecrated ground and any tombstone or monument marking the grave. Nevertheless, one of his last students, Vincenzo Viviani, devoted himself to ensuring that Galileo was not forgotten. He compiled a definitive edition of all of Galileo's works except for the banned *Dialogue*. He also wrote the first biography of Galileo's life. (Viviani died in 1703, but he left instructions in his will and money to construct a tomb for Galileo. Giovanni Battista Foggini completed a tomb in Florence's Basilica of Santa Croce in 1737, and, with the church's consent, both Galileo and Viviani's remains were reinterred there.) Other details about Galileo's life also endure in the surviving letters and writings of Galileo and his circle of friends and enemies as well as in

GALILAEVS GALILEIVS PATRIC. FLOR.
GEOMETRIAE ASTRONOMIAE PHILOSOPHIAE MAXIMVS RESTITVTOR
NVLLI AETATIS SVAE COMPARANDVS
HIC BENE QVIESCAT
VIX. A. LXXVIII. OBIIT. A. CIƆ. IƆ. C. XXXXI.
CVRANTIBVS AETERNVM PATRIAE DECVS
X. VIRIS PATRICIIS SACRAE HVIVS AEDIS PRAEFECTIS
MONIMENTVM A VINCENTIO VIVIANO MAGISTRI CINERI SIBIQVE SIMVL
TESTAMENTO E.I.

Nearly a century after his death, Galileo was finally memorialized with a tomb in Santa Croce, featuring a marble bust staring upward and flanked by female figures that represent Astronomy and Geometry.

official records, such as the files of the Inquisition.

Today, Galileo is recognized as one of the great scientists of all time. He is sometimes called the father of modern science. He even had a spacecraft named in his honor that was launched in 1989 to study Jupiter and its moons. Because of Galileo's work and even because of his treatment by the Inquisition, science began to achieve independence from the influence of philosophy and theology. Scientists of the future turned to instruments, experimentation, mathematics, and data rather than doctrines and tradition to explain the world.

Other scientific revolutionaries joined Galileo in ushering in a new era of scientific and philosophical inquiry and practice. While Galileo was making discoveries that cast doubt on the Aristotelian worldview, the English philosopher Francis Bacon was formulating a new methodology for determining scientific truth. He argued that natural knowledge should be acquired through empirical and rational means—key concepts behind the modern scientific method. René Descartes, the French mathematician, scientist, and philosopher, established the foundations of modern philosophy and made further contributions to the scientific method. In 1533, Descartes had been prepared to publish his book *Le monde, ou Traité de la lumière* (*The World*; also called *Treatise on the Light*), in which Copernicanism is central to his cosmology, but he changed his mind when he heard of Galileo's condemnation. The Scientific Revolu-

GALILEO GALILEI

NASA'S GALILEO MISSION

According to the National Aeronautics and Space Administration (NASA), "Galileo changed the way

NASA's *Galileo* spacecraft sent back revelatory images of Jupiter and its moons, including a 1999 photograph of a volcano, now known as Prometheus, on the Galilean moon of Io.

> we look at our solar system." However, NASA is not referring to Galileo Galilei—NASA's *Galileo* was a spacecraft named in honor of the astronomer himself. Appropriately, the *Galileo* probe, launched in 1989, became the first craft to orbit Jupiter. For eight years, it sent back observations of Jupiter and its moons. These included the four largest moons now known as the Galilean moons—Io, Europa, Ganymede, and Callisto. *Galileo* discovered volcanoes on Io, a liquid ocean under the surface of Europa, and a magnetic field around Ganymede. The *Galileo* probe also caught images of a comet smashing into Jupiter and achieved the first asteroid flyby. In 2003, at the end of the spacecraft's useful life, NASA sent *Galileo* plunging into Jupiter's atmosphere, where the spacecraft broke into pieces.

tion culminated with the work of physicist and mathematician Isaac Newton, whose discoveries transformed how people understood and studied the universe.

In 1744, Catholics were once again permitted to read Galileo's *Dialogue*, although in a slightly censored edition. By 1820, the prohibition on teaching Copernicanism was finally lifted. However, Galileo and Copernicus's works were not removed from the official list of banned books until 1834.

The symbolic conflict between faith and science was finally resolved in 1992, when Pope John Paul II announced the conclusions of a thirteen-year investigation into Galileo's condemnation by a Pontifical Commission. More than 350 years after the trial, the Catholic Church admitted that the rejection of Copernicanism and the subsequent disciplinary measure against Galileo had been an "error of judgment."

Timeline

1564 Galileo Galilei is born on February 15 in Pisa.
1574 Galileo's family moves to Florence.
1575 Galileo studies at the monastery at Vallombrosa.
1581 Galileo enrolls at the University of Pisa to study medicine.
1585 Galileo leaves the university without earning a degree.
1589 Galileo accepts a position as professor of mathematics at the University of Pisa.
1592 Galileo wins a position as professor of mathematics at the University of Padua.
c. 1596 Galileo invents a geometric and military compass
1604 The "new star"—Kepler's supernova—appears in the sky.
1609 Galileo constructs a telescope and begins making astronomical observations.
1610 *The Starry Messenger* is published. Galileo takes position of mathematician and philosopher to the grand duke of Tuscany in Florence.
1612 *Discourse on Floating Bodies* is published.
1613 History and demonstrations concerning sunspots and their properties is published in Italian.
1615 Galileo's *Letter to Castelli* is circulated.
1616 Galileo is warned to abandon Copernicanism,

which is condemned by the Inquisition.

1619 *Discourse on the Comets* is published under the name of Mario Guiducci.

1623 Cardinal Maffeo Barberini becomes Pope Urban VIII. *The Assayer*, dedicated to him, is published.

1624 Galileo visits Rome and meets with Pope Urban VIII.

1632 *Dialogue Concerning the Two Chief World Systems, Ptolemaic and Copernican* is published. Sales of the *Dialogue* are halted by the order of the pope. Galileo is summoned to Rome to stand trial for heresy.

1633 Galileo is condemned and sentenced by the Inquisition. He returns to Florence under house arrest.

1634 Galileo's daughter, Sister Marie Celeste, dies.

1635 The first Latin translation of *Dialogue* is published abroad.

1637 Galileo loses his sight.

1638 *Discourses and Mathematical Demonstrations Concerning Two New Sciences* is published.

1642 Galileo dies at his home on January 8.

Glossary

ADVOCATE To support.

BALANCE An instrument that determines an object's weight typically consisting of a horizontal beam supported at the center with weighing pans at each end. The object being weighed is placed in one pan and objects of known weights are placed in the other.

CARDINAL A priest of high rank in the Catholic Church.

CELESTIAL Pertaining to the sky, heaven, or outer space.

CENSOR To remove parts of a book or other media considered objectionable; also, the official who performs this duty.

COMET An object composed of ice and dust that orbits the sun.

CONDEMN To censure or sentence to a punishment.

CONVENT A community of people belonging to a religious order, especially one made up of women (called nuns).

COSMOLOGY The branch of astronomy that studies the structure and evolution of the universe.

DENOUNCE To condemn or accuse formally or publicly.

DENSITY A measurement of mass per unit of volume.

DISPUTE A debate, controversy, or serious disagreement, especially one that is long-running.

DOCTRINE A set of teachings held by a religious, political, or philosophical organization.

DOWRY Money or property that a bride brings to her husband's family upon marriage.

ERRONEOUS Incorrect or containing errors.

FORTIFICATION The practice of constructing defensive military works, such as walls and towers.

HERESY An action or belief that contradicts orthodox religious doctrine.

HYPOTHETICAL Based on an unproven proposition rather than established truth.

INAUGURAL First or introductory.

OPTICAL Related to the study of light or sight.

ORBIT The path of one celestial body moving around another.

PENDULUM A weight suspended from a fixed point so that it swings freely back and forth.

PENITENTIAL Feeling or exhibiting regret for a wrongdoing.

PHYSICS The branch of science that deals with the nature and properties of matter, energy, motion, and force.

PHYSIOLOGY The study of the functioning and processes of living things.

PROJECTILE An object thrown or propelled forward through the air.

Glossary

PSEUDONYM A fictitious name, often used by an author to hide his or her identity.

REGENT Someone who rules a kingdom in place of a monarch who is too young or otherwise unable to govern.

REINTER To rebury or entomb again.

RHEUMATISM A physical condition in which joints, muscles, and tissue can become inflamed and cause pain.

SUNSPOT A dark area that appears on the surface of the sun.

THEOLOGY A system of religious beliefs and theory.

VEHEMENTLY Forcefully or passionately.

For More Information

ASTROLab
Parc national du Mont-Mégantic
189, route du Parc
Notre-Dame-des-Bois, QC J0B 2E0
Canada
(819) 888-2941
Website: http://www.astrolab-parc-national-mont-megantic.org/en
The ASTROLab is an astronomy activity center devoted to making science accessible. Its virtual museum site "Canada under the stars" at http://astro-canada.ca provides information on astronomy in Canada and in general.

Canada Science and Technology Museum
1867 St. Laurent Boulevard
Ottawa, ON K1G 5A3
Canada
(613) 991-3044
Website: http://www.sciencetech.technomuses.ca
The Canada Science and Technology Museum aims to help the public to understand the ongoing relationships between science, technology, and Canadian society.

The Galileo Galilei Institute for Theoretical Physics (GGI)
Largo Enrico Fermi, 2
50125 Florence
Italy

For More Information

+39 055 275 5255
Website: http://ggi-www.fi.infn.it
The GGI organizes and hosts small-size advanced workshops in theoretical particle physics. The institute is located on the historic hill of Arcetri, near the house where Galileo spent periods of his life and died in 1642.

Hayden Planetarium
American Museum of Natural History
Central Park West at 79th Street
New York, NY 10024-5192
(212) 769-5100
Website: http://www.amnh.org/our-research/hayden-planetarium
The Hayden Planetarium works to educate the public on astronomy and astrophysics. It offers public lectures about the universe by acclaimed scientists and a program that gives an interactive tour of the universe.

Museo Galileo–Institute and Museum of the History of Science
Piazza dei Giudici 1
50122 Florence
Italy
+39 055 265 311
Website: http://www.museogalileo.it/en/index.html
One of the foremost international institutions dedicated to the history of science, the Museo Galileo is home to the

only surviving instruments designed and built by Galileo himself. The museum also holds the scientific collections of the two dynasties that once ruled Florence: the Medici and the House of Lorraine.

Museum of the History of Science
Broad Street
Oxford OX1 3AZ
United Kingdom
01865 277280
Website: http://www.mhs.ox.ac.uk

The Museum of the History of Science houses an unrivaled collection of early scientific instruments from antiquity to the early twentieth century. In 2009, it held a "Galileo in Print" exhibit to mark the four hundredth anniversary of his first telescopic observations.

National Air and Space Museum
Independence Avenue at 6th Street SW
Washington, DC 20560
(202) 633-2214
Website: https://airandspace.si.edu

The Smithsonian Institution's National Air and Space Museum collects, preserves, studies, and exhibits artifacts, archival materials, and works of art related to the history, culture, and science of aviation and spaceflight and the study of the universe.

For More Information

Starry Messenger: Observing the Heavens in the Age of Galileo
Beinecke Rare Book & Manuscript Library
121 Wall Street
New Haven, CT 06511
(203) 432-2977
Website: http://beinecke.library.yale.edu/collections/highlights/starry-messenger-observing-heavens-age-galileo
The Starry Messenger exhibition, which celebrated the International Year of Astronomy 2009, included a selection of engravings, charts, diagrams, and texts related to European observations of the heavens from the sixteenth through the eighteenth centuries. The Beinecke Rare Book & Manuscript Library continues to provide information about the artifacts in the exhibit on its website.

WEBSITES

Because of the changing nature of internet links, Rosen Publishing has developed an online list of websites related to the subject of this book. This site is updated regularly. Please use this link to access the list:

http://www.rosenlinks.com/LOSR/galileo

For Further Reading

Anderson, Michael, ed. *Pioneers in Astronomy and Space Exploration* (Inventors and Innovators). New York, NY: Britannica Education Publishing, 2013.

Andronik, Catherine M. *Copernicus: Genius of Modern Astronomy* (Genius Scientists and Their Genius Ideas). Berkeley Heights, NJ: Enslow Publishers, Inc., 2015.

Demuth, Patricia Brennan. *Who Was Galileo?* New York, NY: Grosset and Dunlap, 2015.

Hightower, Paul. *Galileo: Astronomer and Physicist* (Great Minds of Science). Rev. ed. Berkeley Heights, NJ: Enslow Publishers, Inc., 2009.

Jackson, Tom. *Physics: An Illustrated History of the Foundations of Science.* New York, NY: Shelter Harbor Press, 2013.

Jackson, Tom. *The Universe: An Illustrated History of Astronomy.* New York, NY: Shelter Harbor Press, 2012.

MacLachlan, James. *Galileo Galilei: First Physicist* (Oxford Portraits in Science). New York, NY: Oxford University Press, 1997.

Moore, Peter. *Trailblazers in Science* (Original Thinkers). New York, NY: Rosen Publishing, 2015.

Panchyk, Richard. *Galileo for Kids: His Life and Ideas with 25 Activities.* Chicago, IL: Chicago Review

For Further Reading

Press, 2008.

Principe, Lawrence M. *Scientific Revolution: A Very Short Introduction.* New York, NY: Oxford University Press, 2011.

Richard, Orlin. *12 Scientists Who Changed the World.* North Mankato, MN: 12-Story Library, 2016.

Robinson, Andrew, ed. *The Scientists: An Epic of Discovery.* New York, NY: Thames & Hudson, 2012.

Sís, Peter. *Starry Messenger: Galileo Galilei.* New York, NY: Frances Foster Books, 1996.

Sobel, Dava. *Galileo's Daughter: A Historical Memoir of Science, Faith, and Love.* New York, NY: Bloomsbury USA, 2011.

Steele, Philip. *Galileo: The Genius Who Charted the Universe* (National Geographic World History Biographies). New York NY: National Geographic Children's Books, 2008.

Bibliography

Cowell, Alan. "After 350 Years, Vatican Says Galileo Was Right: It Moves." *New York Times*, October 31, 1992.

Drake, Stillman. *Galileo: A Very Short Introduction.* New York, NY: Oxford University Press, 2001.

Finocchiaro, Maurice A., ed., trans. *The Essential Galileo.* Indianapolis, IN: Hackett Publishing Company, Inc., 2008.

Galilei, Galileo. *Discoveries and Opinions of Galileo* (Translated by Stillman Drake). New York, NY: Anchor House, 1957.

Heilbron, J. L. *Galileo.* New York, NY: Oxford University Press, 2010.

Machamer, Peter, ed. *The Cambridge Companion to Galileo.* New York, NY: Cambridge University Press, 1998.

Naess, Atle. *Galileo Galilei: When the World Stood Still.* New York, NY: Springer, 2005.

NASA. "Galileo Legacy Site." Solar System Exploration, June 28, 2010. https://solarsystem.nasa.gov/galileo/index.cfm.

Reston, James Jr. *Galileo: A Life.* New York, NY: HarperCollins Publishers, 1994.

Rowland, Wade. *Galileo's Mistake: A New Look at the Epic Confrontation between Galileo and the Church.*

New York, NY: Arcade Publishing, 2001.

Sharratt, Michael. *Galileo: Decisive Innovator.* New York, NY: Cambridge University Press, 1999.

Shea, William R., and Mariano Artigas. *Galileo in Rome: The Rise and Fall of a Troublesome Genius.* New York, NY: Oxford University Press, 2003.

Van Helden, Albert, and Elizabeth Burr. "The Galileo Project." Rice University, 1995. http://galileo.rice.edu.

Whitehouse, David. *Renaissance Genius: Galileo Galilei and His Legacy to Modern Science.* New York, NY: Sterling, 2009.

Wootton, David. *Galileo: Watcher of the Skies.* New Haven, CT: Yale University Press, 2010.

INDEX

A

Academy of Florence, 26
Apelles, 61, 62
Archimedes, 14, 22, 24, 58
Aristotelianism, 14, 16, 18, 19, 20, 29, 41, 43, 44, 50, 58, 59, 60, 62, 64, 76, 86, 91
Aristotle, 14–15, 19, 20, 30, 44, 50, 60, 72, 76
  cosmology, 16
  physics, 16, 17, 20, 58–59, 60, 76
Assayer, The, 71, 73, 74
Astronomical and Physical Balance, The, 71, 73

B

Bacon, Francis, 19, 91
balance, 24, 26
Basilica di Santa Croce, 10, 89
Bellarmine, Robert, 33, 56, 64, 66, 67, 68, 80
blindness, 77, 88
Bologna, University of, 26, 31
books, banning of, 67, 81, 89, 94
Borro, Girolamo, 29
Brahe, Tycho, 32, 51
Bruno, Giordano, 32, 33, 64

C

Caccini, Tommaso, 64
Campanella, Tommaso, 32
Capra, Baldassare, 37
Castelli, Benedetto, 62, 69, 77
Catholic Church, 4, 6, 7, 33, 53, 56, 58, 64, 65, 66–68, 77, 78–81, 88, 89, 93–94
Clavius, Christopher, 26, 56
Colombe Lodovico delle, 59
comets, 71, 72–73, 93
Contarini, Giacomo, 34
Copernicanism, 4, 6, 23 43, 55, 58, 62, 64, 65, 66, 67, 68, 71, 74, 76, 78, 80, 81, 85, 91, 94
Copernicus, Nicolaus, 17, 19, 54
Cremonini, Cesare, 44

D

density, 58, 60
Descartes, René, 19, 91
Dialogue, 76–78, 80, 85, 89, 93
Discourse on the Comets, 73
Discourse on Floating Bodies, 59–61

Index

E
Elements, 21, 29
Euclid, 14, 21, 29

F
Florence, importance of to Galileo, 11–13

G
Galen, 20
Galilei, Galileo
  childhood, 8–11
  children, 40, 56
  condemnation by Catholic Church, 4, 6, 7, 67–68, 78–81, 91, 93, 94
  death, 88
  description of hell, 28
  development of the telescope, 6, 45–46, 48
  education, 11, 13, 19–22
  house arrest, 81, 84
  illness, 56, 69, 77, 79, 83, 85
  inventions, 24, 26, 34, 36–37, 71
  legacy, 91–94
  as mathematician and philosopher of the Tuscan court, 53, 56
  and the "new star," 43–44
  parents, 8–11, 12, 19, 22, 30, 31, 69
  planetary observations, 6, 49–51, 53, 54–55, 56, 62
  and sunspots, 6, 55, 61–62, 80
  teaching career, 23, 24, 29–30, 31–34, 39, 41, 43, 46
  written works, 26, 30, 34, 38, 52, 53, 58, 59–61, 62, 64, 65, 67, 71, 73, 74, 76–78, 80, 81, 85, 89, 91, 93
Galilei, Giulia, 8, 69
Galilei, Vincenzo (father), 8–11, 10, 12, 19, 22, 30
Galilei, Vincenzo (son), 40, 56, 69, 88
Galileo spacecraft, 92–93
Gamba, Livia (Sister Arcangela), 40, 69
Gamba, Marina, 39, 56, 69
Gamba, Virginia (Sister Maria Celeste), 40, 69, 81
geocentric model of the universe, 16, 41, 44,

54, 61, 67
geometric and military compass, 36–37
Grassi, Orazio, 71, 72–73, 74
Greek language, 11, 13, 14
Guidobaldo, Marquis del Monte, 26, 29, 31
Guiducci, Mario, 73

H

heliocentric model of the universe, 7, 17, 19, 43, 54, 55, 67, 77, 89
heresy, 6, 33, 64, 65, 66, 67, 68, 79, 81
History and demonstrations concerning sunspots and their properties, 62
Hobbes, Thomas, 89

I

Inquisition, 33, 64, 65, 67, 78–81, 91

J

Jesuits, 56, 62, 72, 74, 81
John Paul II, Pope, 94
Jupiter, moons of, 6, 50–51, 52, 53, 56, 58, 62, 71, 91, 92

K

Kepler, Johannes, 17, 41, 43, 51
Kepler's nova, 43

L

Latin language, 11, 13, 14, 32, 89
Leaning Tower of Pisa, 30, 87
Letter to Castelli, 64, 65
Letter to the Grand Duchess Christina, 65, 89
Little Balance, The, 26
lunar libration, 88

M

Medici, Christina de', 62, 71
Medici, Cosimo I de', 10
Medici, Cosimo II de', 10, 50, 52, 53, 62, 66, 69, 71
Medici, Ferdinando I de', 26, 31, 69, 71, 76
Medici, Ferdinando II de', 10
Medici, Francesco de', 26
Medici family, history of, 10
moon, mountains of, 6, 50
Mysterium Cosmographicum, 41, 43

Index

N
Newton, Isaac, 93

O
On Motion, 30
On the Revolution of the Heavenly Spheres, 17

P
Padua, University of, 23, 31–32, 39, 41, 43
parabola, 87
pardon, of Galileo's Catholic condemnation, 94
Paul V, Pope, 32, 56, 66
pendulum, 22, 38, 87
Pinelli, Giovanni, 31, 32
Pisa, University of, 11, 19, 20, 22, 29, 30, 53, 59
Ptolemy, 16–17

Q
Qualifiers, 67
quintessence, 16, 44

R
Reckoning of Weights for the Balance and the Small Scale, A, 73
Renaissance, 12–13

Ricci, Ostilio, 21, 22

S
Sagredo, Gianfrancesco, 39, 41, 53
Salviati, Fillipo, 58
Sarpi, Paolo, 32, 46
Saturn, rings of, 54
Scientific Revolution, 7, 19, 93
Starry Messenger, The, 51, 52, 58
sunspots, 6, 55, 61–62, 80

T
telescope, 6, 52, 53, 54, 58
  development of, 45–46, 48
thermoscope, 34
tides, 41, 77, 80, 88
Two New Sciences, 85–88
Tychonic universe, 51

U
Urban VIII, Pope, 74, 77, 78, 88–89

V
Venice Arsenal, 34, 87
Venus, phases of, 54–55, 56

ABOUT THE AUTHOR

Corona Brezina has written numerous books for young adults. Several of her previous books have also focused on topics related to science and technology, including *The Scientist's Guide to Physics: Discovering Relativity* and *Newly Discovered Planets: Is There Potential for Life?* She lives in Chicago, Illinois.

PHOTO CREDITS

Cover, p. 1 (portrait), p. 25 Leemage/Universal Images Group/Getty Images; cover, p. 1 (background), pp. 35, 42, 60–61, 86–87 Science & Society Picture Library/Getty Images; pp. 4–5 Leemage/Corbis Historical/Getty Images; p. 9 PHAS/Universal Images Group/Getty Images; pp. 12–13 ullstein bild/Getty Images; pp. 14–15 Museo de Firenze Com'era, Florence, Italy/Bridgeman Images; p. 18 Time Life Pictures/The LIFE Picture Collection/Getty Images; pp. 20–21 Hemis/Alamy Stock Photo; p. 27 DEA/Veneranda Biblioteca Ambrosiana/De Agostini/Getty Images; pp. 28–29, 75 Heritage Images/Hulton Fine Art Collection Getty Images; p. 36 Alinari Archives/Getty Images; pp. 40–41 DEA/Archivio J. Lange/De Agostini/Getty Images; pp. 44–45 Universal Images Group/Getty Images; pp. 47, 49 De Agostini Picture Library/Getty Images; pp. 55, 78–79 Science Source; p. 57 Kean Collection/Archive Photos/Getty Images; p. 63 Galleria degli Uffizi, Florence, Italy/Bridgeman Images; p. 70 Eric Vandeville/Gamma-Rapho/Getty Images; p. 72 Chronicle/Alamy Stock Photo; p. 82 DEA/W. Buss/De Agostini/Getty Images; p. 90 DEA/G. Nimatallah/De Agostini/Getty Images; p. 92 Universal History Archive/Universal Images Group/Getty Image; back cover, pp. 8, 23, 39, 54, 69, 84 agsandrew/Shutterstock.com; interior pages background Ilya Bolotov/Shutterstock.com.

Designer: Brian Garvey; Senior Editor: Kathy Kuhtz Campbell; Photo Researcher: Bruce Donnola